FEAR OF CRIME

NEW OBSERVATIONS

Howard S. Becker, series editor

The close and detailed observation of social life provides a kind of knowledge that is indispensable to our understanding of society. In the spirit of Robert E. Park, the books in this series draw on an intimate acquaintance with their subjects to make important contributions to the development of sociological theory. They dig beneath the surface of conventional pieties to get at the real story, and thus produce ideas that take account of the realities of social life.

FEAR OF CRIME
Incivility and the Production
of a Social Problem

DAN A. LEWIS AND GRETA SALEM

Transaction Books
New Brunswick (U.S.A.) and Oxford (U.K.)

Second Printing, 1988.
Copyright © 1986 by Transaction, Inc.
New Brunswick, New Jersey 08903

Library of Congress Catalog Number: 85-31827

ISBN: 0-88738-086-7

Printed in the United States of America

Library of Congress Cataloging in Publication Data

Lewis, Dan A.
    Fear of crime.

    Bibliography: p.
    Includes index.
    1. Crime and criminals—United States—Public
opinion. 2. Public opinion—United States. 3. fear.
4. Social control. I. Salem, Greta. II. Title.
HV6791.L47   1986   364'.973   85-31827
ISBN 0-88738-086-7

Contents

List of Tables and Figures

Tables

Figures

Acknowledgments

This book is a product of the Reactions to Crime Project (1975-80) conducted at the Center for Urban Affairs at Northwestern University between 1975 and 1980. Much of the data reported here were collected during those years, and our approach was shaped by the people we collaborated with during that time. We are especially appreciative of the assistance received from Ron Szoc and Mike Maxfield who did much of the statistical analyses reported in the pages to follow. Judy Lieberman was very helpful in the analysis of the qualitative data. The project was supported by the National Institute of Justice as part of their Research Agreements Program. Richard Barnes and Winifred Reed acted as liaisons between the project and the funding agency and were instrumental in the success of the project. Their support and understanding were of great value to us. Louis Masotti and Margaret Gordon served as directors of the Center during this period, and their encouragement made our work easier. There was a group of researchers at the Center that collaborated in ways not often found in the academy. In particular, Fred DuBow and Wes Skogan brought their intelligence and general good will to the cooperative efforts that led to the successful completion of the project and ultimately to this book. There were many others who worked on this project and assisted us on this book. Howard Becker, Al Hunter, Wally Goldfrank, and Paul Lavrakas gave needed encouragement and criticism that strengthened the effort. Indeed, the book has emerged over the past ten years as a dialogue with those who have been working in this field.

We wish to acknowledge the love and support of our spouses, Dick and Stephanie, and our children, Susanne, Peter, Erica, and Matthew for their general interest and help. Erica also contributed her expert editorial advice. Special thanks go to the people in the ten communities we studied, for without their openness and good will this project would not have been possible. We hope that our efforts are useful to them.

Finally, while we gratefully acknowledge the assistance of those who strengthened the book, we alone are responsible for its flaws.

This work was partially supported under Grant Number 78-NI-AX-0057 from the National Institute of Justice, U.S. Department of Justice. The survey reported upon in this volume was supported in part by Grant Number R01MH29629-01 from the National Institute of Mental Health to the Center for Urban Affairs. Points of view or opinions in this document are those of the authors and do not necessarily represent the official position or policies of the U.S. Department of Justice.

Introduction

The study of social problems is always complicated by definitions. What is a social problem? Who decides? How do you know it's there? Is there an objective standard that can be applied to all situations or are social problems defined comparatively? There is even disagreement as to how important these questions are to the study of social problems. Some scholars see these questions as essential and problematic while others see them as marginal and routine. The importance of these definitional issues hinges on one's view of the social world. If that world is seen as a *given,* a reality out there in which we all participate, the problems associated with *inter-subjectivity,* the capacity to understand and judge the experiences of others, are seen as unimportant. If that social world is seen as an artifice, a construction, then social problems are created by men and women and their nature is problematic.

These matters are of no small import to the study of social problems. Indeed, those who see definitional issues as central focus, on the claims various groups and interests make about social problems. Because they see the study of social problems as the examination of that claim-making process, they pay little attention to the real pain and suffering experienced by the victims of the problematic behavior under consideration. (Spector and Kitsuse, 1977.) Those who see the definitional issues as marginal, because social problems are obvious and their definition commonsensical, focus on the measurement of the problem, its prevalence and solutions. They, however, frequently fail to see the multidimensional nature of the problem which stems from the varying perspectives from which it is viewed.

Recent critiques of the former position have pointed out that the emphasis on definitions renders the behavior that is problematic to a secondary status. What "counts" is how that behavior is defined, not how it is experienced. The result is an analysis that denies the experience of those who behave badly and those who must cope with that behavior. To reduce the study of social problems to the claims of interest groups is to lose the dimension of social life through which the problematic behavior is manifested. That dimension is often filled with citizens who bear the burden of our social problems, both as perpetrators and as victims.

This is not to dismiss the definitional issues. Lemert (1951) distinguishes between the problematic behavior people exhibit and the social responses to it by defining the former as primary and the latter as secondary deviation. Piven (1981) points out that most contemporary sociologists have emphasized the secondary and treated the primary deviation as of marginal interest. Outside of academic sociology, however, the emphasis in the last decade has been on the *primary deviation,* as if society's and the state's responses are of little significance in the emergence and persistence of the problematic behavior.

To completely ignore the task of coming to terms with what Wirth (1940) has termed the *evaluational elements* in the study of social problems, however, means never asking who decides what behavior or situation is to be defined as a social problem. Wirth recognized over forty years ago the essentially reflexive nature of study in this area.

> There is a widespread belief that the problems of maladjustment of men to one another and to the world in which they live arise out of the nature of men or of things. Despite the work of a long line of social scientists who have indicated that the situations we call social problems are problematical only because they represent deviations from socially accepted norms and expectations, there is substantial evidence to indicate that even some contemporary sociologists continue to deal with social problems as if they did not involve evaluational elements. [Wirth 1940:472-73]

Gusfield used the metaphor of container and contained to distinguish between the social problem and its public construction. This metaphor recognizes the interaction of two realities that combine to produce a social problem for the consideration of both researcher and policy makers. The one is a set of conditions that can be identified and interpreted; the other is a theoretical framework, a range of interests or an ideological orientation that draws attention to particular relationships between sets of phenomena and turns attention away from others. The two are interdependent and deeply entwined.

The analysis of the social problem fear of crime in this book is based both on our recognition of the reflexive nature of social science and on our understanding that there is a phenomenon that exists independently of the various ways in which it is interpreted and defined by scholars. Fear of crime exists; we know it from our own experiences and those around us. However, how that fear is conceptualized and understood is dependent on the categories of thought brought to bear on its analysis. Although there are no right or wrong definitions and interpretations of this social problem, there are differences in the extent to which an analysis captures the experiences and perceptions of those who are fearful. To the extent that one container captures an experience better than another, there will be differences in the effectiveness of the policies designed to remedy the problematic conditions.

The studies of and policies directed at the problem of fear of crime illustrate well the impact of conceptualization on the experience of everyday life. In the chapters that follow, we will argue that the recent literature, which has been dominated by what we call the *victimization perspective,* has failed to come to terms with the anomalies in its research findings, due in part to the way in which the research problem has been constructed and interpreted. This perspective, often implicit in the major studies, treats fear of crime as a response to victimization. It assumes that urban residents are fearful primarily because they have either been victimized themselves or they have heard about the victimization of others.

We will argue, on both theoretical and empirical grounds, that this approach is too narrow and that, by focusing only on the psychological responses to a victimization, it fails to take into account the political and social structures within which such fears are shaped and nourished. We do not assume that individualistic psychological perspectives are without utility. We do believe, however, that they are too restrictive to account for the ways in which urban residents relate and respond to their neighborhood environments.

We approach the study of fear of crime from what we call the *social control perspective,* which is adapted from the *Chicago School* orientation to the study of the city and urban community life. We will argue that fear is more than a response to a particular victimization event. Rather it is a consequence of the erosion of social control as it is perceived by urban residents. Thus, we see the fear of crime problem in much the same terms as Wilson sees the urban problem in general, namely, as the erosion of order within the local community.

> What these concerns have in common, and thus what constitutes the "urban problem" for a large percentage (perhaps a majority) of urban citizens, is a *sense of the failure of community.* When I speak of the concern for "community," I refer to a desire for the observance of standards of right and seemly conduct in the public places in which one lives and moves, those standards to be consistent with, and supportive of, the values and lifestyles of the particular individual. Around one's home, the places where one shops, and the corridors through which one walks there is for each of us a public space wherein our sense of security, self-esteem, and propriety is either reassured or jeopardized by the people and events we encounter. [Wilson 1975:24].

We will argue in the pages that follow that fear of crime is not always triggered by direct experience with or knowledge about criminal events. Fear, we believe, appears also to be elicited by what we have labeled *incivility*—those features in a community that reflect the erosion of commonly accepted standards and values. In those communities where citizens develop the capacity to regulate behavior in conformance with those conventional standards, fear will be held in check. Our analysis, in the end, emphasizes the importance of collective action in response to social change. Fear becomes a social problem when collective action is difficult and social change is rapid and devastating.

In the following chapters, we (1) trace the development of fear of crime as a social problem and the dominance of the victimization perspective in its analysis; (2) trace the history of and delineate the major components of the social control perspective; (3) apply that perspective in the analysis of data on fear of crime collected in ten neighborhoods in Chicago, Philadelphia, and San Francisco; and (4) compare and discuss the policy implications we associated with the two conceptualizations of the problem.

1

The Emergence of Fear of Crime as a Social Problem

Until the late 1960s the study of crime was viewed primarily as the question of why criminals violate laws. Researchers sought to understand the motivations of those engaged in criminal activity, and social policy planners developed programs grounded in that research and designed interventions to change those motivations.

Two theoretical explanations for the emergence of crime and delinquency were particularly influential in determining the shape of crime prevention programs. Edwin H. Sutherland's theory of *differential association* described crime as a function of value conflict between groups. In the third edition of *Principles of Criminology,* published in 1939, Sutherland depicted criminal activity as the result of the socialization to values of one group, which clashed with the values of a more powerful group in society.

In contrast, Robert Merton in "Social Structure and Anomie," published in 1938, developed a *strain theory,* which argued all members of society generally share the same values. Deviance followed from the differential distribution of legitimate means to achieve those values. For example, all young men consider the achievement of wealth an important goal. The poor, however, lack the means (e.g., education, employment opportunities, and so on) for obtaining that goal and, therefore sometimes utilize illegitimate means (e.g., criminal activity) to gain it.

Merton and Sutherland agree, however, that the critical factor in explaining criminal activity is social position. Criminal activity is a learned behavior that is transmitted by a local subculture. And although Merton's analysis draws our attention to the differential opportunities available to adolescents in the community and Sutherland's to the interaction between peers, both see social status as the fundamental concept for the analysis of the crime problem. Offending behavior is produced by one's position in the social structure or by socialization into a deviant subculture.

1

The focus on social status and opportunity structure was further developed in Cloward and Ohlin's (1960) *Delinquency and Opportunity,* which was used to orient the planning of programs for delinquency prevention at the Ford Foundation and the President's Committee on Juvenile Delinquency (Marris and Rein 1967). The authors, arguing that adolescents in poor areas resorted to illicit activities to achieve such goals as status, wealth, and recognition, identified the crime problem as one of differential access to commonly held values. The "solution" that followed from this analysis was clear. Access to these values would have to become more readily available to adolescents who did not have the means to achieve them because of their position in the social structure.

The culprit in this analysis, interestingly enough, was not the social structure that shaped opportunity, but rather the bureaucracies which served the poor.

> The processes of assimilation were breaking down, and could only be repaired by an enlargement of opportunities, but this emancipation would only come about as enabling institutions of assimilation—the schools, the welfare agencies, the vocational services—recognized their failure, and became more imaginative, coherent, and responsive. [Marris and Rein 1967:53].

This analysis sees the city as an essentially neutral or benign background within which prevention strategies are to be developed. Urban society is viewed "essentially as a benevolent anarchy in which all competing groups could participate in the struggle" (Marris and Rein 1967). The disadvantages confronted by the poor could be mitigated by social welfare agencies that would provide the support required to help them compete for scarce resources. "The will to compete is primary and social agencies are to be judged, above all by their ability to foster and sustain it" (Marris and Rein 1967).

The delinquency prevention projects at the Ford Foundation and the President's Committee identified bureaucratic reform as their goal. These programs called for comprehensive planning and bureaucratic cooperation in a world assumed to be without conflicting groups or interests. The problem of bureaucracy was to be solved by creating new bureaucracies infused with a previously lacking self-awareness and an experimental mentality. Thus, crime prevention was to be achieved by a bureaucratic reform that would make it possible for the disadvantaged to achieve the goals the culture has socialized them to desire.

The failure of these programs to solve the crime problem was attributed by some critics to an inadequate analysis of the issue. Particularly important in this regard was the failure of the analysis to recognize that opportunity was, in fact, shaped by the larger structure of the metropolis, and that bureaucracies were not capable of self-renewal.

By the late 1960s, the soaring crime rate and the ghetto riots turned the attention of policymakers away from the criminal and toward the victim. The so-called backlash, reflected in public anger at the infusion of funds into the Black community and at the concern with the rights of the criminal rather than those of the victim, led to an interest in alternative approaches to the crime prevention problem that would give primary consideration to the behavior of those who are threatened by criminal activity.

Instead of examining the motivation of the perpetrator, the questions raised concerned the impact of crime on the life of the victim and the community at large.

> Predatory crime does not merely victimize individuals, it impedes and, in the extreme case, even prevents the formation and maintenance of community. By disrupting the delicate nexus of ties, formal and informal, by which we are linked with our neighbors, crime atomizes society and makes of its members mere individual calculators estimating their own advantage, especially their own chances for survival amidst their fellows. [Wilson 1975: 21]

The *cost of crime* (Miller 1973) went beyond what the victim might lose. It involved rather the subsequent fear of crime of both the victim and those aware of the victimization. This fear appeared to generate behavior that was, in fact, destructive to the community. Thus, the fear of crime became as much of a social problem as the crime itself.

Surveys revealed that close to 50 percent of the adults living in urban areas were afraid to be out at night in their own neighborhoods. The media portrayed individuals crippled by fear and limited in their freedom to lead normal productive lives. And government agencies responded at the federal, state, and local levels by funding and implementing a wide range of programs designed to reduce fear of crime among selected populations. Indeed, some commentators labeled fear of crime as one of the principle causes of the decline of city life.

At the same time, the research community moved from a consideration of the causes of crime and the motivations of the perpetrator to an examination of the effects of crime on victims and potential victims and on their attitudinal and behavioral reaction to the threats that confronted them.

Initially the research interest in fear developed as a concomitant of an interest in assessing the "true" amount of crime in our society. The early studies funded by the National Commission on Crime and the Administration of Justice attempted to determine both the level of crime and the level of fear Americans experience. The primary interest of these scholars was in assessing *the dark figure* of crime, that is, those unreported and underreported crimes whose magnitude was not reflected in the official crime statistics of police departments.

Attention in these early studies was primarily focused on index crimes such as rape, murder, burglary, robbery, and assault. Fear was considered mainly because it was assumed that levels of fear would be congruent with the true amount of crime in an area.

Biderman, Reiss, and Ennis set the tone for the scholarship on fear of crime in the 1970s. Each of them administered surveys published in 1967 and funded by the President's Commission on Law Enforcement and the Administration of Justice to randomly selected populations. While the surveys varied in their focuses, all attempted to measure the amount of fear reported by respondents. Fear, while measured differently in each survey, was implicitly defined as anticipating the occurrence of a criminal event. Where anticipation was high, fear, by definition, was assumed to be high. An increase in crime, it was anticipated, would generate an increase in fear. All three researchers took as their task the documentation of the level of fear among respondents, assuming always that fear was related to the amount of crime to which respondents were exposed. Indeed, given the measures employed by scholars, it would have been impossible to dissociate fear of crime from the anticipated criminal events. For example, Biderman measured fear of personal attack by one item:

> Would you say there has been an increase in violent crimes here in Washington? I mean attacks on people—like shootings, stabbings and rapes? Would you say that there's now very much more of this sort of thing, just a little bit more, not much difference, or that there is no more than five years ago? [1967: 132, see also Appendix D: 11]

To report an increase in violent criminal events is to score high on fear of crime (or in this case, attack). Reiss, while avoiding a direct discussion of fear, subsumed the topic in a more general discussion of "citizen perceptions about crime in their areas." Here again anticipation of the criminal event was synonymous with fear.

> When you think about your chances of getting robbed, threatened, beaten up, or anything of that sort, would you say your neighborhood is

(compared to other neighborhoods in town): very safe, above average, less safe, or one of the worst? [Reiss 1967:33-34].

Have you changed your habits because of fear of crime? (stay off streets, use taxis or cars, avoid being out, don't talk to strangers). [1967:102-110]

These early studies highlighted two ways in which victimization could increase fear. The *individual fear profile* approach focused on the correlates of fear among demographically defined groups. Emphasis here was less on the criminogenic aspects of the environment and how it was assessed and more on the demographic characteristics associated with victimization and fear of crime. This approach relied on large national samples and was generally descriptive.

The *neighborhood assessment* approach focused on the amount of crime the respondent expected the local neighborhood to produce. Both Ennis (1967) and Biderman (1967) developed measures of fear that were premised on the imputed relationship between a dangerous neighborhood and individual fear. Biderman called this measure an *Index of Anxiety*, and it was composed of the following items:

1. What was it about the neighborhood that was most important?
   (This was asked only of those residents who indicated the neighborhood was more important than the house in selecting their present residence.) Safety or moral reasons vs. convenience, and so forth.
2. When you think about the chances of getting beaten up would you say this neighborhood is very safe, about average, less safe than most, one of the worst?
3. Is there so much trouble that you would move if you could?
   (Again, a screen question asked only of those who did not say their neighborhood was very safe.)
4. Are most of your neighbors quiet or are there some who create disturbances? (all quiet, few disturbances, many disturbances)
5. Do you think that crime has been getting better or worse here in Washington during the past year? (better, worse, same) [Biderman et al 1967:121]

Ennis (1967) distinguished between *Fear of Crime* and *Perception of Risk*. He measured fear by the following items:

1. How *safe* do you feel walking alone in your neighborhood during the day?
2. How *safe* do you feel walking alone in your neighborhood after dark?
3. How often do you walk in your neighborhood after dark?

4. Have you wanted to go somewhere recently but stayed home because it was *unsafe*?
5. How concerned are you about having your house broken into? [Ennis 1967:72-75].

Risk was measured by two items:

1. How likely is it a person walking around here at night might be held up or attacked—very unlikely, somewhat likely, somewhat unlikely, or very unlikely?
2. Compared to other parts of the city, is a home or apartment around here much less likely to be broken into—somewhat less likely, somewhat more likely, or much more likely to be broken into? [Ennis 1967:75-76]

Ennis distinguishes between feeling unsafe (the report of fear) and the assessment of the possibility that a crime will occur (risk); but his fear measure seems as much an assessment of the neighborhood as it is a report on the respondent's sense of unease.

As Baumer (1977) has pointed out, there is little published information on how these early measures were developed. But for our purposes it is their content rather than their methodological limitations that is of interest, for these early scholars developed the research vocabulary for the study of fear of crime in the decade that followed.

The importance of this early work, for our purposes, can be found in the assumed association between fear (as a reported internal state of the individual) and the number of victimizations the respondent anticipates. Fear is assumed to be a consequence of the potential for victimization, and the research issue is how that fear is distributed within a given population. The neighborhood is seen as a setting within which that victimization takes place. If the respondent scores high as an *anticipator* of victimization, he is defined as fearful. A neighborhood is fear inducing to the extent that it provides a context for criminal activity.

This approach to the analysis of fear of crime, which we shall label the victimization perspective, postulates "crime" as an event that is experienced by the individual as either a direct or indirect victim. Accordingly, fear is a consequence, a response in time, of having had contact with criminal events. If direct victimization fails to account for particularly high levels of fear, then indirect contact, usually through the media or personal communication, is postulated as the mechanism through which the experience of crime affects the individual. Fear then becomes an indicator of the effect of victimization on the individual. It is seen as a consequence of exposure to crime. This scenario, however, assumes a direct linearity that has rarely been tested.

Indeed, the early findings of the research have raised some real questions about this relationship. Although a few studies reported positive relationships between victimization and fear (Feyerhern and Hindelang 1974; Kleinman and David 1973). The early work of Biderman, Reiss, and Ennis as well as much of the subsequent research (McIntyre 1967; Boggs 1971; Conklin 1971; Fowler, McCalla, and Mangione 1974; Hindelang, 1974) reported findings that demonstrated the lack of concordance between fear levels and experience.

For the most part, the researchers found that fearful persons greatly outnumbered those who had been exposed to victimization. Furthermore, there was a significant range of variation in fear levels in those neighborhoods generally acknowledged to be unsafe.

The Law Enforcement Assistance Administration (LEAA) Victimization Surveys, which measured fear levels among various demographic groups in the intercity comparisons, found that fear of crime and victimization experiences were not necessarily congruent. Indeed, fear of crime was often more prevalent among those groups (i.e., the elderly) least frequently victimized (Skogan 1976). While young Black males consistently reported the largest number of victimizations and the least amount of fear, older females (both Black and White) reported the highest level of fear and the lowest number of victimizations.

Scholars have attempted to explain this apparent paradox by employing more sophisticated analytical techniques to the analysis of crime and the levels and dimensions of fear reported by respondents. Some have postulated the existence of various social-psychological mechanisms to rationalize their findings. For example, Stinchcombe et al. (1977) introduced the concept of *vulnerability* to help explain fear among women and the elderly.

The most commonly relied upon mechanism is the idea of *fear of strangers*. Faced with the disjunction between levels of fear and levels of victimization, several scholars introduced the *stranger* as the stimulus of fear. As stated by Ennis:

> It is not the seriousness of the crime, but rather the unpredictibility and the sense of invasion by unknown strangers that engenders mistrust and hostility. [1967:80]

McIntyre (1967:40) echoed the same thinking in her analysis of avoidance behaviors. "The precautions which people take to protect themselves indicate that underlying fear of crime is a profound fear of strangers. "Biderman (1967) saw the relationship as being even more direct: "fear of crime is the fear of strangers." And Skogan (1977) interpreted the relationship between robbery victimization and fear as a consequence of the fear of strangers. But the fear of strangers is only introduced *ex post facto* to interpret results and explain findings. While Skogan may have been correct in attributing the relationship between robbery and fear to an intervening fear of strangers, that suggestion was pure conjecture. The fear of stranger explanation posits the existence of an intervening type of fear which has not been measured. Consequently, this attribution process is not opened to empirical testing and has no better standing than victimization itself as an explanatory factor (Blake and Davis 1964:460).

There has been some progress made within the victimization perspective by refining measurement techniques and analytical procedures in particular. Furstenberg (1971), Fowler, McCalla and Mangione (1974), Skogan (1976), and Hindelang, Garofalo and Gottfriedson (1978) all refined the conceptualization of fear within the victimization framework. Distinctions between fear, concern, worry, and risk have helped distinguish the various attitudinal dimensions captured in the idea of fear, and these clarifications have improved the explanatory power of more recent studies.

Also, refining the various types of victimization (personal/property, single/multiple, direct/indirect, and so on) used as the independent variable has led to improved results. In this vein, some scholars have attempted to develop more refined methods of measuring the amount of crime to which respondents are exposed. Balkin (1979:343), for example, argued that "fear of crime is a rational response to the actual incidence of crime, and that where discrepancies appear it is because of faulty objective measures of crime incorrectly calibrating the real risk of crime."

Skogan (1977), Garofalo (1977), and Hindelang *et al.* (1978) have all made valuable contributions to our understanding of fear of crime from the victimization perspective. Indeed, the last decade has seen much progress since the early formulations of Biderman (1967), Reiss (1967), and Ennis (1967). Many of the difficulties of the earlier work may be overcome by this second generation of scholars who have expanded the perspective rather than rejecting it.

However, the analysis of the victimization perspective, which assumes implicitly that fear levels can be explained by victimization experiences, remains basically unsubstantiated. This analysis shares one important feature with the strain and subcultural theories used to explain criminal behavior, and this feature is the basis of the perspective's weakness. The victimization perspective offers an implicit theory of motivation. Fear is explained in terms of the stimuli (victimizations) that trigger the fear in the individual. Just as Sutherland and Merton (and those who followed in their footsteps) sought to explain the motivations of offenders in terms of the values of the groups to which they belonged, so the victimization scholars seek to explain fear of crime in terms of how victimization experiences generate fear in individuals. Victimizations lead to fear just as naturally as working class cultures lead to delinquency.

In each instance there is a linear relationship assumed between motivation and subsequent behavior. However, as we noted earlier, the programs based on the analysis of criminal behavior failed to lead to a reduction in crime. And the analysis of fear based on the victimization perspective has yet to account for the inability of researchers to discover adequate evidence for the assumed linear relationship.

Accordingly, some scholars have begun to expand the consideration of the variables involved in the generation of fear of crime. Garofalo and Laub, for example, note the following:

> All of the factors discussed above—the ambiguous relationship between victimization and the fear of crime, the indications that crime is not generally perceived as an immediate threat, and the mixing of fear of crime with fear of strangers—point to the conclusion that what has been measured in research as fear of crime is not simply fear of crime. [1979:246]

Biderman suggests that an understanding of fear of crime might need to take into consideration factors that are not directly associated with individual victimization experiences.

> We found that attitudes of citizens regarding crime are less affected by their past victimization than by their ideas about what is going on in their community—fears about a weakening of social controls on which they feel their safety and the broader fabric of social life is ultimately dependent. [1967:160]

More recently, Hunter identified other forces in the community that might engender fear.

> Fear in the urban environment is above all a fear of social disorder that may come to threaten the individual. I suggest that this fear results more from experiencing incivility than from direct experience with crime itself. [1978:9]

The *incivility* in Hunter's remark does not refer to specific situations or events that can be seen across neighborhoods. Rather, it is descriptive of a variety of circumstances which suggest to neighborhood residents that all is not well in their communities. These situations vary with the interests, values, and resources characterizing various neighborhood populations. They may involve unacceptable behavior by teenagers; physical deterioration in homes, commercial areas or public spaces; the intrusion of "different" population groups into the area; or an increase in marginally criminal behaviors such as drug use and vandalism. Although the events or conditions captured in the incivility term may vary in each neighborhood, they elicit the same concern among area residents that the mechanisms for exercising social control are no longer effective, and the values and standards that in the past characterized the behavior of local residents are no longer in force. In each instance, long-time residents in the community felt they could no longer predict what might confront them upon leaving the security of their homes. The order on which they had depended had been violated in some way and their neighborhoods were no longer dependable places in which to live.

The notion that fear may well be related to contextual factors in the environment is reminiscent of an older tradition in the analysis of crime developed by the scholars associated with the sociology department of the University of Chicago in the 1920s and 1930s. We examine their arguments next in our effort to provide some guidelines for the study of fear of crime, which moves beyond the linear relationships assumed in the victimization perspective and accounts also for the context in which the fear is engendered.

2

Fear of Crime and Community Context

The idea that contextual variables might help explain behavior grew out of the social control perspective formulated in the 1920s by the Chicago School sociologists. They sought an understanding of the changes taking place in urban communities and the strategies used by inhabitants to accommodate themselves to the pressures of city life. The social control perspective they formulated is both a general social theory and, at the same time, a theory of social problems. Born of a concern with social order in a time of great social change, the perspective attempts to show how the growth of cities created social problems that were less the result of individual pathology and more a consequence of urban social forces. Therefore, the study of urban society was seen in large measure as the study of social change and the social problems that followed.

The Chicago School took as its central dilemma the problem of order in an industrialized society. In this respect it shared the concerns of European thinkers at the turn of the century who saw the decline of community and the order it produced as their central dilemma. If custom, tradition, and kin attachments no longer bonded citizens, how was social order possible? While Toennies and Durkheim extended the evolutionary tradition into the twentieth century to answer this question, a group of scholars at the University of Chicago drew upon the metaphors of natural history and biology to counter the pessimistic theorizing of European scholars. Reformist in temperament, these men were developing tools to study the fast growing metropolis shooting up around them and the changes taking place in local urban communities. Led by Park, Burgess, and McKenzie, whose *The City* was published in 1925, the scholars formulated an approach to the study of society that for the next twenty-five years dominated the new academic discipline of sociology. Borrowing from the evolutionary thinkers a concern about social change and the nature of community, these scholars sought to examine the changes taking place in the structure of the local communities and to determine when residents were adapting to the pressures of city life.

11

Park, Burgess, Wirth, and others focused on understanding the effect that urbanization (as a particular variant of social change) was having on city dwellers, particularly the newly arrived poor European immigrants. From that theorizing emerged the notion that crime was the "natural" result of the process at work in cities, and urban communities faced serious problems in maintaining social control in the face of these processes. The conceptual link between social change and social control was the concept of *social disorganization*.

Members of the Department of Sociology differed in how they operationally define the concept of social disorganization. Thomas and Znaniecki (1939) were among the first to discuss how communities and families became disorganized under the pressure of city life. Park specified a process of organization, disorganization and reorganization as the capacity to regulate social life reemerged. A number of scholars (Landesco 1929; Shaw and McKay 1942) treated the disorganization as an "objective" judgement about the state of the community. However, all the researchers utilizing the concept of *social disorganization* agreed that city life disrupted the local social order (Carey 1975).

In his analysis of the processes at work, Wirth (1938) showed how increases in the density, heterogeneity, and size of the urban population increased mobility, insecurity, and instability. This then led to the establishment of formal control mechanisms designed to mitigate the personal disorganization caused by city life. For social change in the city affected local communities in a variety of ways, disrupting social control and introducing forms of deviance (including crime and delinquency) as a consequence of that disruption.

Carey gave us a good working definition of social disorganization.

> A socially disorganized community is one unable to realize its values. The consequences of disorganization (delinquency, dependency, desertion, truancy, high rates of mental illness, etc.) are considered undesirable by most of the citizens who live in the disorganized community— they would do something about them if they could. The characteristic response to the question, "disorganized from whose viewpoint?" was "disorganized from the viewpoint of the people who live there." [1975:107]

Social control is "the means of doing something about them" and, as such, plays a pivotal role in how the major social forces of city life effect the social organization of local communities.

> The close living together and working together of individuals who have no sentimental and emotional ties fosters a spirit of competition, aggrandizement, and mutual exploitation. To counteract irresponsibility and

potential disorder, formal control tends to be resorted to. [Wirth 1938:15]

Given this general set of factors, the social and cultural institutions at the local or neighborhood level are not capable of performing their socialization and social control functions and, therefore, criminal activity follows. Families, churches, friends, and neighbors cannot counter the dysfunctional influences of the city that lead to social disorganization and criminal activity in the urban community.

> It is probably the breaking down of local attachments and the weakening of restraints and inhibitions of the primary group, under the influence of the urban environment, which are largely responsible for the increase of vice and crime in great cities. [Park 1970:25]

Primary face-to-face relations, which had been the basis of social control in less complicated societies, are inadequate control mechanisms in the context of the urbanization process (Smith 1979). This is especially true for second generation immigrants (those born in the United States) who feel less tied to the traditions of the old country (Wirth 1933) and are pulled towards the deviant values of the metropolis.

Crime within this theoretical orientation is the direct result of the pressures of city life. Rather than being an aberration due to individual character disorder, it is an anticipated consequence of the effects of disorganization on the local community. A theory of the city "explains" criminality; as city life disorganizes local communities, crime increases.

A major source of the social disorganization process was the *invasion* of business and industry.

> Under the pressure of the disintegrative forces which act when business and industry *invade a community*, the community thus invaded ceases to function effectively as a means of social control. Traditional norms and standards of the conventional community weaken and disappear. Resistance on the part of the community to delinquent and criminal behavior is low, and such behavior is tolerated and may even become accepted and approved. [Shaw, et al. 1929:24]

This notion of *invasion* offers an interesting, if underdeveloped, insight into the process that makes crime a problem for a neighborhood (Snodgrass 1976; Molotch 1979). This invasion implies the introduction of exogeneous influence into the life of the community. Shaw hypothesized that as business and industry expanded into residential areas, it weakened traditional norms. Land originally used and controlled by residents was now controlled by businesses; this transfer of land destroyed in some unspecified ways the operative social controls. This hypothesis was developed in the 1920s in Chicago when the central business and commercial district was expanding. The influence of Burgess' concentric zone theory is evident in Shaw's approach (Burgess, Lohman, and Shaw 1937). The intrusion of business into residential areas caused crime by undermining the instruments of social control.

The solution to the crime problem posited by the Chicago scholars draws upon their general theory of urbanization, social control, and social disorganization.

> The distinctive features of the urban mode of life are often seen sociologically as consisting of the substitution of secondary for primary contacts, the weakening of bonds of kinship and the declining social significance of the family, the disappearance of the neighborhood and the undermining of the traditional basis of social solidarity. [Wirth 1938:21]

Against this setting, the individual is forced into *voluntary associations* to achieve his ends.

> Being reduced to a stage of virtual impotence as an individual, the urbanite is bound to exert himself by joining with others of similar interests into organized groups to obtain his ends. This results in the enormous multiplication of voluntary organizations toward as great a variety of objectives as there are human needs and interests. [Wirth 1938:22]

Thus, crime could be reduced if local communities reasserted the primacy of their values over the insidious influences of city life. The voluntary association is particularly well suited to achieve this end.

In 1934, Clifford Shaw and Henry McKay applied their theoretical constructs to the design of the Chicago Area Project, a practical application informed by a series of books on delinquency published in the same period (e.g., Shaw and McKay 1942; Shaw et al. 1929). Leaving the classroom, these scholars introduced a series of interventions into Chicago neighborhoods designed to remedy social disorganization by the reintroduction of new mechanisms of social control.

The project "attempts to deal with crime as a natural phenomenon," and focuses on the local community as the place to take action.

> The essential logic of the Area Project becomes, then, one of discovering the pertinent social processes and significant cultural organization of the

community as expressed in the institutions of local residents themselves, and through these, introducing values consistent with the standards of conventional society. [Burgess, Lohman, and Shaw 1937:23]

The prevention of crime is a matter of working through and with local people and institutions to strengthen the community's capacity to enforce "values consistent with the standards of conventional society."

> If juvenile delinquency in the deteriorated areas is a function of the social life characteristics of these situations, it seems that a feasible approach to the solution of the problem would be to effect constructive changes in the attitudes, sentiments, codes, and moral standards of the neighborhood as a whole. [Burgess, Lohman, and Shaw 1937:22]

The Chicago Area Project thus was seen as a mechanism for reasserting social control. "Society has here an opportunity to discover and encourage forces which will make the local community, insofar as is possible, independently effective in dealing with its own problems" (Burgess, Lohman, and Shaw 1937:23). Key to the effectiveness of the project was the enlistment of indigenous leadership to work through local institutions in the fight against crime. This emphasis on voluntary participation at the neighborhood level as a method for reasserting local values are central, given a definition of crime as the process of value erosion. Only by combatting social disorganization (as indicated by delinquency and crime rates) could local communities become safer places to live.

Crime could be prevented if the community changed itself. The destabilizing force of urbanization could be mitigated by local action. Thus, the link between crime prevention and community, forged conceptually over forty years ago, was based on a theory of social disorganization that defined urbanization as the culprit that weakened social control and left the individuals adrift. Crime was one of many negative outcomes of this process, and it followed from the theory that preventing crime was a function of strengthening the local community in its attempt to assert social control. The emphasis on voluntary associations and local citizen action followed from an analysis of social bonds that emphasized the importance of primary social relations over the secondary relations manufactured in the metropolis. Crime could be curbed only if social institutions rather than criminal justice institutions (courts, probation, police, and so on) were strengthened. To prevent crime, the impact of city life has to be mitigated by the strengthening of socializing and controlling institutions in the community. Crime was one of many social problems that surfaced on the face of social disorganization. Indeed, one of the weaknesses of the social control perspective was its incapacity to specify the types of deviances that would appear in different circumstances.

The social control perspective was challenged in the early 1940s by the new theories of deviance discussed in Chapter 1, which emphasized motivational and socialization factors to account not only for the origins of deviance, but also for its persistence and differentiation (Merton 1938; Sutherland 1939). A substantial critique of the social control perspective focused on the theoretical and methodological inadequacy of the idea of social disorganization that followed the invasion (Carey 1975). Seen by some as a class-biased value judgment concerning different cultures (Mills 1943), and by others as a vague and poorly operationalized concept, social disorganization became discredited.

Building on his own work in *Street Corner Society* (1943), Whyte emphasizes the newly created social bonds in immigrant communities.

> If social disorganization involves a "decrease of the influence of existing social rules," and the rules referred to are those of the peasant society from which the immigrants came, then the slum is certainly disorganized. However, that is only a part of the picture. It is fruitless to study the area simply in terms of the breakdown of old groupings and old standards; new groupings and new standards have arisen [Whyte 1943:38].

Rather than focusing on the destructive forces in the community, emphasis was placed on the institutions, habits, values, and norms that constituted the newly emerging moral order.

> For too long sociologists have concentrated their attention upon individuals and families that have been unable to make a successful adjustment to the demands of their society. We now need studies of the way in which individuals and groups have merged to recognize their social relations and adjust conflicts. [Whyte 1943:34]

Mills (1943) challenged the criteria social scientists were using in assessing these communities as disorganized. In his review of social problem textbooks, he observed a bias that stemmed from the white, rural, protestant, and nativist backgrounds of the scholars. That background colored their understanding of urban, immigrant life. Social disorganization was nothing more than the deviation from norms these men held to be correct, and that judgement had been couched in scientific terminology. Both Whyte and Mills demonstrated that what the social control perspective described as *deficiencies* in community life were nothing more than *differences* in social organization.

What evolved in those World War II years was less a concern about studying deviance within the social control perspective and more an interest in understanding the social organization of community life. The interest in the achievement of value integration and regulation remained, but the emphasis was on describing the variations in social organization that could be found in urban communities. This generation of researchers was particularly concerned with social cohesion in communities with mixed ethnic and racial compositions. By the 1960s researchers turned their attention to the negotiated nature of many of the social and cultural configurations of urban life and away from the primordial sentiments and attachments of displaced peasants in new world contexts. As scholars began to examine what happened between as well as within ethnic groups, the shifting relations between ethnic and racial groups became an important factor in the study of fear of crime.

An important stimulus to this kind of analysis was Janowitz's (1952) concept of the *community of limited liability*. As this concept suggests, the community ceases to be the all encompassing and pervasive influence on individual life. Rather, it's meaning and influence is tempered by the position of the individual urban residents. For some the residential community becomes less important than other networks. For others, home owners and parents of small children for example, the community remains a major resource and force for social control. Thus, individuals *invest* in local community when local institutions meet their needs. As these needs change, however, adults concern themselves less with the local conditions and the future of the community.

The influence of this transformation can be seen most directly in the work of Gerald Suttles (1968). His examination of the impact of racial and ethnic succession on community life reintroduces the concept of invasion. In Suttles' analysis, however, it is population movement rather than the intrusion of business and industry that most directly changes the shape and composition of the local community. And in his description of ethnic conflict and accommodation, he illustrated the strategies used by local residents in their effort to maintain social control.

Each ethnic section of the Addams area differs from the other in the extent to which it possesses a standardized routine for managing safe social relations. There is, however, a general agreement upon the social categories beyond which associations are not pursued. The boundaries of the neighborhood itself form the outermost perimeter for restricting social relations. Almost all the residents caution their wives, daughters, children, and siblings against Roosevelt, Halsted, Congress, and Ashland. Within each neighborhood, each ethnic section is an additional boundary which sharply restricts movement. [1968:225]

Suttles argues that fear and isolation are minimized to the extent that "standardized routines for managing safe social relations" exist. Thus, potential conflict between mutually suspicious ethnic groups is kept in check by what he called *ordered segmentation*. Each ethnic group maintains social control within the prescribed boundaries where access can to some extent be controlled. The groups with greater economic and political resources maintain that control. Those who lack the resources are less effective in this regard.

Although Suttles resembled the Chicago School scholars in his focus on local resources and local control, he differed in his approach to community. Whereas the Chicago scholars sought to combat invasion by restructuring the local institutions of the entire community, Suttles described an approach that combatted invasion by limiting the size of the community to the area that could be controlled.

Thus, the community of limited liability becomes a community by limiting liability. And invasion, rather then disorganizing communities, provides a stimulus for their reorganization on a smaller scale. Synthesizing the classic social control approach with Whyte's critique and Janowitz's down-to-earth notions of attachment, Suttles describes how community is created through its response to outside challenges. Community residents have their personal liability limited through these protective initiatives. The threat of disorder from without sustains the order within. This order does not rely on primal sentiments for its cohesive power, but rather on the need to reduce conflict between groups. Political and governmental activities are of secondary importance in ordering and controlling behavior. It is the "invisible hand" of ordered segmentation that maintains social control. The ability to maintain that control, however, is dependent upon the capacity of each community to modify, if not control, access to the area it inhabits.

Although there are clear differences in the work of the social control theorists of the 1930s and those of the 1960s and 1970s, it is the similarities in their arguments that provide the guidelines that help shape our investigation of fear of crime. The earlier critics of the Chicago School rejected the notion of an objectively defined social disorganization. Suttles and the other more recent researchers identify different invasion forces and strategies for maintaining and reinstituting the moral order in the communities. All of the scholars agree, however, that community context has an impact on the attitudes and behaviors of urban residents. They also agree on a "solution" to the problems associated with social change in urban communities. Where they diverge is on the basis of the bonds forged through social control. The earlier theorists argue for an effective bond and the later group for a self-interested link.

These two approaches will be incorporated into our research design as we examine fear of crime in ten neighborhoods located in three major urban centers. Our analysis will be guided by an assumption that the motivational theories implicit in both the strain theories of criminal behavior and in the victimization approach to the study of fear of crime, need, at a minimum, to be supplemented by an approach that takes the urban context and the community into account. We reject, however, the notion of an objectively defined notion of community social disorganization and substitute for it the less pejorative context of incivility, which reflects a characterization of the social concept generated by the local residents. We also emphasize the involvement of the indigenous population in solving the problems associated with social change in urban communities and treat secondary institutions as peripheral.

There is, of course, a tradition in which secondary institutions (police, courts, and corrections) are treated as central. In that political tradition, *civility* is not merely a condition present or absent due to social processes; rather, it is an intentional *political* construct created by the purposeful activity of *citizens* through their institutions and the obligations they instill. Some philosophers have gone so far as to argue that the primary purpose of the state is to ensure civility, or as Hobbes called it *civil peace,* and that government legitimacy in democratic societies rests on the ability to maintain that peace while preserving individual liberty. Zweibach (1975) argues forcefully that politics makes civility or civilization possible and that when self-governance fails, social disorganization follows.

Because the sociological literature revolves around the notions of community and social change in the city, there is a noticeable absence of thought about government and politics. The social control theorists have emphasized the role of what they call primary institutions in the maintenance of order. City government and the politics of the community are treated as secondary matters that do not effect social control. However, to address the issue of social control without thinking about the role of political institutions is to give a partial analysis of the problem. If the social control approach has utility for the analysis of fear of crime, then we should look at how political institutions regulate the behavior of people. From Shaw and McKay through Suttles, the pursuit of order is *depoliticized*. This is true at both the normative, philosophical level and at the empirical, descriptive level. It is as if order in the city had nothing to do with politics, citizenship, and the state. The city seems to exist outside the nation-state in a realm of pure social relations guided by custom, tradition, and norm.

The explanation for this oversight can be found in the distinction between primary and secondary institutions. The world of politics is the world of secondary institutions, a world which has little hold on the activities of city dwellers. Without the primary ties of community and family, the sociologists argue, disorder is inevitable. Government is at best reactive and at worst irrelevant to civil peace. Thus, the formal attempts to order relations within the polity are defined out of the serious discussion of social control.

Yet most political theorists see legal institutions and the norms surrounding them as the building blocks of self-regulation. Indeed, modern society makes government essential to civil peace. This blind spot among the sociologists has led to gaps at the normative and descriptive levels in their explanations of the social control process. The state has as one of its first priorities the attempt to maintain peaceful social relations. Democratic theorists see the production of order with liberty as the *sine qua non* of the legitimate state. Indeed the primary purpose of government for many theorists is the production of orderly social and economic relations. Politics is the realm of negotiation of how we live in relative peace and security. Many political theorists focus the debate on the obligations that would allow citizens to live together in harmony under the legitimate coercion of the government. They ask what set of obligations are legitimate and acceptable to the governed, and how will these rules be arrived at by the people who will have to live with them.

The purpose of government is to create civility, that is, a kind of environment that will serve to avoid the disorganization that makes civilization impossible. This capacity to create a common life must be developed. Civility is not easily produced. It demands a constant concern with the how and why of public life. For the sociologist this is the business of mutual accommodation. But for many of us, government is the first place we turn to solve the problems of incivility. We look to the state through the police to create the civility we seek. We make laws that enhance the common values that lie below that civility. The notion of consent and obligation are not far from the idea of civility, for they provide the bedrock for the common expectations we hold. We must look to the realm of politics to understand the mechanisms that people use to produce civility and the order that most see as the *sine qua non* of civilization. Creating that order is what we expect of democratic government.

Civility is then a political concept. The order that it suggests does not spring mechanically from the community, rather, it is something we try to create in order to preserve what we care about. Needless to say, there are divisions over what should be preserved and what should be changed, and that is precisely the area where politics come into play. The state is the arena where the ideas about how that order should look and what values ought to flourish compete. There is competition for what the contours of the civility should look like.

This is especially true of the competition for how problems that challenge the civility of the community should be handled. Often changes in communities herald shifts between racial and ethnic groups. As residents of urban communities work together to preserve civility or reverse incivility, they are drawn to the political arena both descriptively and normatively. The task of combating incivility means taking political action in both the sense that citizens must agree on which values are worth preserving, what Zweibach calls the *common life,* and make demands of governmental agencies (police, courts, and so on) for improved services.

In this struggle groups look to the state to preserve civility. We seek the order that makes social relations possible through state action and the obligations of citizenship. Those citizens with the fewest personal resources have to depend the most on these institutions for protection. Any explanation of social control must come to terms with state action in the quest for order, not only because empirically the state is involved in so much that passes for social control, but also because normatively the state seems to many to be the best way to develop coercive methods of self-regulation. The state may be a poor replacement for the traditions and customs of the past, but it is the one we depend on the most.

An attempt was made to reduce the conflict between ethnic groups by creating police departments. The original purpose of the police department was to reduce disorder. The department's capacity to do this was limited by the norms that dictated what they could and could not do. Keeping the peace was a limited goal that excluded more intrusive attempts to limit individual liberty. The prison system is another institution that owes its existence to the pursuit of order. Unsuccessful as it might be, prison was meant to serve as a deterrent to breaking the law. Indeed, the whole idea of the criminal who sinned against the state rather than against another person put the state in the role of the aggrieved party when there was conflict between people.

If community organizations are to play an important role in social control, that role will emerge only through accommodation with the state apparatus. This is true both empirically and normatively. As we will show in the pages that follow, the community organizations that were most effective in regulating behavior were those that had developed relations with the state agencies which help to maintain an acceptable level of civility in their communities. While it may be that the representativeness of the governmental apparatus has come into question in the last fifty years, especially in the city, there can be little question about how important the state is to the preservation of order. If fear of crime is basically the fear of disorder, then the politics of civility is the key to reducing fear and understanding its dynamics.

Sociologists look for order in the social relations that precede state action. Political theorists see order produced through the political process. These are both partial views. Social control resides in both the political and social arenas depending on a complicated set of factors that we will describe in the following pages.

3

An Empirical Application of the Social Control Perspective: Fear of Crime in Ten Urban Neighborhoods

Introduction

In order to assess the impact of community context on the attitudes and behaviors of local residents, we needed to look at a number of different types of urban communities. But because so many of the questions we were asking were exploratory in nature, they necessitated the in-depth, unstructured, time-consuming, interview techniques associated with field research. We were thus limited in the number of communities we could examine. In applying the social control perspective, therefore, we utilized the comparative case study method, which allowed us to combine the diversity required for meaningful comparative analysis with the in-depth investigation demanded when a search for alternative theoretical frameworks is initiated.

Our examination of fear of crime within the context of varying neighborhood settings was conducted in ten urban neighborhoods. Four of these are located in Chicago: Wicker Park, Lincoln Park, Back of the Yards, and Woodlawn. Three are in Philadelphia: South Philadelphia, West Philadelphia, and Logan. And three are in San Francisco: Mission, Visitacion Valley, and Sunset. These neighborhoods were neither randomly selected nor meant to be representative of the cities in which they were located. Rather, they were chosen because they represented the range of those neighborhoods typically found in large urban settings and because they offered considerable diversity in crime rates and in the socioeconomic class and racial composition of the population.

In the following chapters, we will present the data to support our argument that variations in the fear of crime, the self-report by citizens that they are afraid, cannot be explained only by directly experienced victimization or the knowledge about the victimizations of others, but must also take into account a number of characteristics associated with the communities in which they live. Thus, in this study the community becomes the unit of analysis, and characteristics typifying each neighborhood become the independent variables associated with the dependent variable—fear of crime. This approach allows us to capture the contextual imprint of local conditions on reported fear levels, which is lost when the research focus is only on the motivations of individuals in demographically defined subgroups.

In the discussions that follow, we will argue that varying fear levels in the study sites can be accounted for in part by the failure of local institutions to exert social control. That is, in those communities in which a large number of residents exhibit fear of crime, local institutions appear to be incapable of controlling neighborhood changes perceived by long-term residents as threatening to the integrity of their community. These might well include changes in the crime rate and in the perceived security in the area. But they may also involve changes in the composition and size of the population, in physical upkeep, in the provision of amenities and services, and in the number and range of problems characterizing the neighborhood. These changes are perceived by local residents as signs of incivility. Because they reflect a change in standards and values, they damage the moral order of the community and suggest that the organization of the community is in disarray. Neighborhoods vary, however, not only in the incivilities confronted, but also in the ability of the residents to deal with them. We identify as sources of social control those resources that residents bring to bear in combatting neighborhood problems and in defending the local moral order. Our analysis of the ten neighborhoods in this study will, therefore, focus on those forces associated with social change, social disorganization, and social control.

In putting these concepts into operation, we will use perceptual rather than objectively measurable indicators. We do this not only because of the difficulty involved in devising adequate measures, but mainly because the attitudes we are studying are based on perceptions rather than on some commonly accepted definition of the situation in each of these areas. Furthermore, we want to avoid the possibility of imposing our own definitions on respondents who might not share them. In putting our concepts into operation and in selecting our indicators, we have tried to approximate as closely as possible the circumstances in which the residents in the neighborhoods conduct their daily affairs.

In considering social change, we will try to assess the extent and the direction of change (better or worse) and the time frame within which it occurs, and we will look at the factors associated with that change. These include changes in the behavior of groups indigenous to the area, the intrusion of new groups or business into the area, or the implementation of new policies by private and public agencies effecting neighborhood development.

Research Sites: The Three Cities

Because an analysis of a community context must take into account the character of the city in which it is located, we begin this section with brief characterizations of Chicago, San Francisco, and Philadelphia. Although they represent diverse sections of the country, each of the three cities serves as the core of a major metropolitan area and each is losing both population and employment opportunities to surrounding suburbs. Chicago and Philadelphia each have a large industrial base, much of which is moving out of the region as well as the city. San Francisco is more of a clean industry town with a heavy emphasis on banking, finance, and tourism.

The members of the large working class population in Chicago and Philadelphia identify strongly with the neighborhoods in which they live. In some cases these are still ethnically and racially homogeneous and constitute *defended spaces* from which *different* population groups and *threatening* businesses are excluded. San Francisco, on the other hand, is known as the city of the avant garde, with a high tolerance for a number of diverse and generally considered deviant life styles.

All three cities reported crime rates that were substantially higher than those of the nation as a whole during the study period (Skogan and Maxfield 1980). However, there were also significant differences between them. Not only were the rates in San Francisco higher than those in Chicago and Philadelphia, but there was an increase in crime reported in San Francisco, while in the other two cities there was a decline. San Francisco's robbery rate was higher than Chicago's by one-third, and both its assault and robbery rates were twice as high as those in Philadelphia where reports of crimes in all categories were the lowest for the three cities. Official crime rates, however, are considered somewhat less than representative of the actual criminal events occurring in a given area, both because of differences in police reporting practices and because of the failure of many victims to notify the police. However, the Law Enforcement Assistance Administration conducted victimization surveys, considered more reliable as indicators of the pervasiveness of crime, in the three cities during the study period. These revealed a distribution similar to that reflected in the official reports.

Neither official rates nor the findings of victimization surveys, however, tell us much about the salience of crime. The visibility of crime in any given city is only partially determined by the criminal events that occur there. Equally important are media decisions to cover crime stories and the determination of local leaders to put crime on the political agenda. Crime was a salient political issue in San Francisco and Philadelphia during the study period. In Chicago, however, the political structure and neighborhood orientation of the city defused crime as an issue by localizing it (Podelefsky and DuBow 1980). The Democratic organization that controlled political life kept crime off the political agenda.

Violent crime in San Francisco was highlighted during the study period by the bizarre *zebra* killings, the kidnapping of Patty Hearst, and the assassination of the Oakland school superintendent. Transcending socioeconomic lines, violent crime hit the poor and the wealthy alike, leading the mayor to note, "there are no safe neighborhoods now." Politically, crime was used as an offensive issue by the opponents of the mayor, the controversial liberal sheriff, and the police chief.

In Philadelphia crime was a politically defensive issue used by the former police chief, who became mayor on a law and order platform, to deflect critics. In Philadelphia crime was also closely associated with race. The mayor's opponents saw the emphasis on law and order as a mask for what they perceived to be his racism and his failure to deal with the crime and gang problems that were disproportionately affecting the Black communities. In contrast to San Francisco where the crime debate focused on specific events and possible deterrent strategies, crime in Philadelphia was a symbolic issue used primarily for purposes of political rhetoric.

The newspapers in all three cities gave crime ample coverage. In a content analysis of eight metropolitan daily newspapers conducted during the study period, Gordon et al. (1979) found an average of six violent crime stories per issue. Half of all the crime stories dealt with homicides. The San Francisco papers, however, gave by far the most extensive coverage. On any given day they reported two to three times as many violent crime stories as those in Philadelphia and half again as many as Chicago (Gordon et al. 1979). Although one might suspect that this coverage reflected the higher crime rate in the area, the fact that San Francisco papers covered more out-of-town crimes than the other papers supports the findings of most media researchers that newspaper coverage of crime reflects not so much the frequency of criminal events, but rather editorial decisions about allocations of news space (Gordon et al. 1979).

Although the cities serving as locales for the study sites exhibited some differences in crime rates, the saliency of crime as a political issue the coverage of crime by the metropolitan newspapers, and the attitudinal responses of their citizens were strikingly similar. In a series of sample surveys conducted by the U. S Census Bureau for the Law Enforcement Assistance Administration of fear levels in twenty-six American cities during the 1972-1974 period, these three cities clustered just above the average for all twenty-six cities in the study. In the 1977 survey, on which this report is based, the same similarities were revealed. (See Skogan and Maxfield 1980 for more details.) Major differences in levels of fear did not characterize the residents of the three cities in this investigation. These differences were found instead in the neighborhoods both within and between cities. And it is to these neighborhoods that we now must turn.

The Neighborhoods

In delimiting the neighborhoods for this study, we were guided by Hunter and Suttles' definition of community: "that piece of urban geography for which residents have a collective awareness which may be manifest minimally in symbolically shared names and boundaries" (Hunter 1974). Boundaries for our study sites thus were determined on the basis of the perceptions of area residents interviewed during the field work phase of the project and were not drawn to match any convenient preexisting geographical subunits. The demographic characteristics of the population in each of the ten neighborhoods are presented in Table 1.

Six of the neighborhoods are considered by the residents in each of the cities to be racially homogenous. The populations in Lincoln Park (Chicago)
and Sunset (San Francisco) are primarily White and middle class. Back of the Yards (Chicago) and South Philadelphia are predominantly working class neighborhoods. Woodlawn (Chicago) and West Philadelphia are populated mostly by low-income Blacks. Four of the neighborhoods are racially and ethnically heterogeneous. Visitacion Valley (San Francisco) is relatively affluent middle and working class population with an average income similar to that of the populations in Lincoln Park and Sunset. The residents in the other integrated areas, Wicker

TABLE 1
Demographic Characteristics

	Lincoln Park	Wicker Park	Woodlawn	Back of Yards	West Phila.	South Phila.	Logan	Mission	Sunset	Visitacion Valley
% Employed	71.8	54.8	44.4	62.2	54.7	52.3	63.6	72.7	64.4	63.8
% Unemployed	9.1	14.4	16.9	12.2	17.3	17.1	16.0	14.7	7.5	9.2
% over $20,000	29.3	12.8	16.4	14.8	10.6	11.0	7.7	14.1	28.8	25.7
% under $10,000	22.6	32.4	29.2	19.6	33.6	29.9	35.0	34.4	20.9	20.5
Mean # Children	.63	1.28	.83	1.30	.84	.85	1.27	.56	.46	.96
% Black	8.1	14.7	95.9	21.0	89.7	18.7	56.8	8.9	2.8	27.1
Age %										
11-20	4.0	12.3	6.0	9.0	10.0	5.4	7.7	6.9	7.8	10.5
21-40	69.0	56.0	43.0	51.0	46.3	48.9	61.0	66.2	50.7	46.1
41-60	18.0	23.0	28.4	28.0	25.9	33.0	23.6	17.6	24.7	32.2
61+	8.0	8.0	22.0	12.0	17.8	12.7	7.7	8.3	17.6	14.3
% Spanish	12.8	32.1	0.0	16.6	.3	1.4	3.8	17.2	2.6	11.3
% Own Homes	22.4	35.0	16.9	42.8	60.4	69.0	65.7	17.5	53.1	67.0
1970 Population	21,329	43,081	53,814	64,761	42,005	105,141	52,494	51,870	41,700	12,083
1975 Population	20,773	37,216	46,759	58,859						

Park (Chicago), Logan (Philadelphia), and Mission (San Francisco), are more economically deprived.

While demographic characterizations facilitate the classification of our research sites, they tell us little about the diversity of the people within them or the physical settings they confront in their everyday lives. For this we turn to the more detailed descriptions that follow.

Middle Class White Communities: Lincoln Park (Chicago) and Sunset (San Francisco)

Lincoln Park is a prototypical *gentrified* neighborhood. In the 1950s and 1960s it was considered a *declining* area. A general decline in the area due to deteriorating housing, conservation of dwelling units and deferred or minimal maintenance was typical. However, urban renewal transformed the neighborhood so that it now is a stable, predominantly white, and predominantly wealthy area. The two neighborhoods covered in the field work are the two western areas of Wrightwood and Sheffield. The former is a middle class neighborhood with many older, white residents working in the trades or middle management. Although poor schools drove many of the younger families out of the area, a new group of young people who are said to be dedicated to the community and have similar socio-economic characteristics to the estblished older residents has been moving into the neighborhood. Most of the residential structures are two and three flats. There is very little new development and no vacant property in the area. Many Wrightwood residents own multiple properties in the neighborhood.

Sheffield, immediately south of Wrightwood, has changed considerably in the last ten years. Extensive renovation and new housing has attracted a more affluent professional class. The area is primarily residential with commercial activity restricted to two major commercial strips. Most of the Sheffield buildings were built in the 1880s just after the Chicago fire. The streets are lined with trees, and many of the buildings are decked with turrets, gables, and stone carvings.

The concentration of large institutions in the community—five hospitals and a major university—has given the question of institutional expansion prominence in the neighborhood and, along with the commercial and adult entertainment spots in the area, has generated traffic and parking problems for the residents. All five of the hospitals have announced expansion plans in the last few years.

The population in the two Lincoln Park neighborhoods is predominantly White with a little over 25 percent in the upper income bracket. A little over 9 percent of the residents are unemployed. One quarter of

them are college graduates, 19 percent have had some college education, and 15 percent have done postgraduate work. However, in spite
of the high income and educationl levels, a large majority of the
residents are renters. The 20 percent home ownership in the area
reflects the high number of young professionals who are not yet ready
to establish themselves permanently.

Not surprisingly, the neighborhood is perceived as a desirable place
to live. None of the respondents characterized their neighborhood in
negative terms. Older residents point to the improvements in the
neighborhood in the last ten years since "the less responsible people
have moved out and the more responsible people have moved in."
Many see the area as a special place. This neighborhood is different
from other Chicago areas. "We are a close community."

In the Wrightwood area, particularly, the residents know and take
care of each other. "We are a close community. Kids know what to do
and where to go if there is trouble," said one parent explaining the
block parent program, which designates with a sign in the window one
house in each block as a place where children can go if they are
harassed or otherwise in trouble. One finds also the suspicion of
strangers typical in close communities. "When we see strangers, we
call each other to see who they are and if they have a right to be there."

Although the relationships in Sheffield are not as watchful, this area
is also considered "a great place to live." The neighborhood is characterized as organized and strong. The people are friendly and congenial.

Sunset is a relatively isolated area in the western portion of San
Francisco. It is generally known as a "nice White, middle-class neighborhood." The residents in this well maintained area are primarily civil
servants, skilled craftspeople, and merchants. The 1970 census data
showed 28 percent of them earning over $20,000. A somewhat smaller
proportion, 21 percent, earned under $10,000, and 7 percent living in
this neighborhood were unemployed. Large numbers of middle-aged
and older people (42 percent are over forty) have raised children and
plan to remain.

Housing is divided between single family (67 percent) and two-story
flats. A little over half of the inhabitants own their homes. The
residents are variously described as conservative, bigoted, and isolated; and, although Sunset has the lowest crime rate of all the San
Francisco sites, the large number of gates on the homes with side
entrances suggests that there is in the area some measure of concern.

Sunset has been characterized as an "isolated, alone place." People
value their privacy and frequently fail to communicate with each other.
At night Sunset is not well lit. The street lights are dim and the lights

from the homes are blocked out by shades and shutters. A field worker noted during an evening walk that "the area seemed abandoned and we felt that if something were to happen, no one would help. They were so "gated up." One organization staff member noted, "there is such individualism; people don't talk to each other."

Working Class and White: Back of the Yards and South Philadelphia

Back of the Yards is a large residential, commercial, and industrial community located west and southwest of the old Chicago stockyards. Housing is varied. Single family homes, two-story walk-ups and four-story apartment buildings are found together in all neighborhoods. There are no high-rise apartment buildings and no public housing units. A few vacant lots are scattered throughout residential developments, but no neighborhood has a high concentration of them. Homes in the area are old, but usually tidy and well kept. Most of the sidewalks and streets are clean and in good condition. About half of the buildings are owner-occupied, and many of the rental properties are owned by residents in the area. Few of the houses are worth more than $30,000. Although a number of single family homes were built in the mid and late 1950s, there has been little new residential construction.

Service industries are scattered throughout the area and the general residential character of the neighborhood is dotted with commercial strips that cut through the community along the major arteries. Major businesses include a large department store, several chain food stores, and several banks. There are also a number of smaller neighborhood groceries, meat markets, and clothing stores. Although the stockyards were closed in 1959, industrial concerns maintain offices and buildings in the old stockyards area. Most of the stockyard land, however, remains vacant despite redevelopment plans. Trucking and railroad shipping have become more prominent in the area since the closing of the stockyards, but most of the area residents appear to be employed outside the community. The area has been the home of immigrants and first generation citizens working in the stockyards since the nineteenth century. Poles, Mexicans, Irish, Germans, Lithuanians, Ukranians and others are all represented in the area. Mexicans are the most recent group to be integrated in the area. One respondent estimated that approximately 25 percent of the owner-occupied housing belongs to Mexicans. For most Mexicans, the Back of the Yards area is the second area of settlement, attracting the more established working class who can afford to leave Pilsen, which serves as the entry point for many Mexican immigrants. Over the past ten years Blacks, who constitute about 21 percent of the area's population, have moved into the area. They have not, however, been integrated into the community and the section to which they are moving is losing White residents. The neighborhoods are clustered around ethnic parishes, and although the ethnic conflict characterizing the area in the early 1930s is no longer prevalent, people identify many of the neighborhoods and blocks with the ethnic groups dominating the area.

According to the 1970s census, a little over 20 percent of the primarily working class residents are in a higher income bracket (over $20,000). Another 24 percent earn under $10,000. Twelve percent of the population is unemployed. Forty-two percent of the households are owner occupied. Thirty-four percent of the residents have not completed their high school education, and 5 percent have college degrees.

Many view the neighborhood as a kind of protected enclave. "We're a little pocket here protected from a lot of problems because we're cut off from the city by the expressway, factories and government buildings." The neighborhood is frequently compared to a small town. People are friendly and open. They are proud of the neighborhood. Groups of teenagers with nothing to do are not usually visible in this area. Consequently, even the elderly feel comfortable and safe.

South Philadelphia is a predominantly White, working class community. Although Italians are clearly dominant in the area, other racial and ethnic groups are represented. Irish, German, and Jews appear to be scattered throughout the White areas. Black residents, who constitute about 16 percent of the area's population, are distributed in checkerboard pockets among the White neighborhoods. Residents appear to identify with these local, ethnic communities rather than the larger neighborhood of South Philadelphia. Racial boundaries are rigidly drawn and form battlelines few residents dare to cross. Racial bigotry appears to be pervasive. And although most respondents consider South Philadelphia a basically safe area, neither Whites nor Blacks feel safe in the other's territory. Black parents, for example, refuse their children access to recreational activities in White sections of the community; white parents similarly restrain their children.

Gangs are not considered a serious problem in the area. Although there are many groups of teenagers congregating on street corners, most respondents consider them relatively harmless "street corner groups," much like those to which they belonged in their youth. There are, however, reports of Black and White gang confrontations. The major White gang in the area, the Counts, has been labeled the "closest thing to a teenage vigilante group that you can get." Their goal is to keep Blacks out of their neighborhoods, and they appear to have the support of their parents and other community residents.

For the most part, the neighborhood is well maintained. The White, Italian areas are particularly impressive. Streets are clean and attractive, lined with old but well-kept row houses. Many families put a lot of effort into remodeling their homes, many of which have tiny gardens infront and small, yet well-kept yards in back.

The residents in the White, Italian neighborhoods form very close communities. People stick together, are very clannish, and tend to be suspicious of strangers. Single-family homes make up 79 percent of the housing in the area. Almost 70 percent of the homes are owner-occupied. One real estate man claimed that values were relatively high in the area because people were buying more than a house, they were buying a *neighborhood*.

This strong community identity appears to be a major resource for the residents of South Philadelphia. Individual resources are few. The residents are basically lower and working class. Seventeen percent are unemployed. Thirty-one percent have no high school diploma, and 29 percent have incomes under $10,000 (1970 figures).

Black residents in the area have even fewer individual resources and, in addition, lack the support that a close community provides. The Black enclaves are not as well maintained as the White areas. Deteriorated and abandoned housing is more pervasive. In general residents claim that the city provides fewer maintenance services to Black communities. The projects in particular present a stark contrast to the White communities. There one typically finds abandoned and boarded up apartments, badly maintained exteriors and littered grounds. Blacks and Whites alike perceive the projects as dangerous and undesirable.

Low Income and Black: Woodlawn and West Philadelphia

Woodlawn is a *ghetto slum* community in the southeast portion of Chicago. Although there are some scattered blocks with single-family and two-flat homes, the majority of buildings in the area are multiple-unit apartment buildings. They are usually run down and deteriorated in appearance. There is no public housing in this area; however, there are two new housing complexes that provide housing for low- and moderate- income groups. These complexes were built and are managed by the dominant neighborhood group in the area, the Woodlawn Organization. Although this housing is for the most part in better condition, there have been some maintenance problems—which reached a climax when the child of an organization staff member was killed in a fall from a defective back porch.

Residents of the area note the differences between West Woodlawn, where there are more elderly and some middle-income residents with well-maintained buildings, and East Woodlawn, where most of the problems exist. However, even in East Woodlawn one notes differences on a block by block basis. On several occasions the field worker described her travels through one block of littered, vacant lots and boarded up, abandoned buildings, followed by a block of well-maintained two-flats and neat lawns. "It was like I was walking in a different world."

The commercial areas are dotted with vacant lots, boarded up stores, taverns, and a few stores that are heavily grated with iron gates. Most respondents feel that stores in the area have low-quality goods for which they charge high prices and, therefore, tend to do their shopping elsewhere.

The dearth of business in the area is reflected in its unemployment rates, which are especially high (50 percent) for youths between 16 and 19 years of age. In 1970 approximately 30 percent of the population lived below the poverty level and approximately 25 percent was on public aid. Of those residents who are employed, more than two-thirds are classified in the blue-collar and service occupations.

Over 95 percent of the residents are Afro-Americans. Thirty-four percent of the residents have no high school diploma, 33 percent are high school graduates, and 3.6 percent have college degrees.

Although Woodlawn exhibits virtually all of the characteristics of a deteriorating neighborhood, some of our respondents were optimistic about its future. The feeling seems to be that the worst is over. The neighborhood has too many assets in its location and the amenities provided by transportation, proximity to the beach and a large park to be permanently disabled. This optimism was reflected by one resident who believed "that Woodlawn will be a highlight of the city in a few years." Others see lots of problems, but insist that the people who care will improve the area. An organizer for the Woodlawn Organization finds that "the feeling of hopelessness that used to plague the area is slowly disappearing. I think people who are living here really feel that there is a future in Woodlawn." Many residents are said to have a high investment in the neighborhood because they have no where else to go.

This vision of Woodlawn is not unanimous. There are others who perceive it as a "desperate community," a "dead end offering nothing to the young people," and "a jungle housing people who deal in drugs and violence." There appears to be evidence supporting both the images presented.

West Philadelphia is one of the oldest Black areas in Philadelphia.

The racial composition of the community began to change in the 1950s when it was a predominantly White, Jewish area. The Blacks who first moved into the area were more similar in social class status to the Whites than those who came in during the late 1960s when the housing projects were built. One middle-aged pharmacist who had lived in the area all his life described West Philadelphia as a "typical middle class, politically active, predominantly Black community."

Most of the dwellings (73 percent) are single-family homes, either detached or row houses. Over half (60 percent) of these are owner occupied. The housing varies in its upkeep, with some of the neighborhoods being extremely well maintained and others less so. One does not get the impression, however, that the maintenance situation is out of control, as in ghetto neighborhoods such as Woodlawn. Although residents complain about the public housing projects, which are low-rise and on scattered sites, the field worker noted that there was no graffiti and the outside of the buildings seemed fairly well cared for.

There are three major commercial areas with primarily small retail businesses, banks, and take-out stands. Mom and pop grocery stores can be found throughout the area, and bars occupy many of the corner locations. In the commercial areas, as in the residential ones, there are a number of vacant buildings and lots. The major physical problem in the area seems to be abandoned housing and vacant lots, which serve as symbols of the physical erosion of the community.

Individual resources are limited. According to the 1970 census, 22 percent of the population lack high school diplomas. Over 17 percent are unemployed, and one-third of the residents have annual incomes under $10,000.

Although some of the elderly respondents characterized the area as "unsafe" and "bad," most felt that West Philadelphia was "nice all over." One elderly respondent reflected the feeling of many of the more active people in the neighborhood when he said "a man couldn't ask for a nicer neighborhood than this."

Ethnic and Racial Diversity: Mission, Visitacion Valley, Logan and Wicker Park

Mission is distinguished among all San Francisco neighborhoods by the quantity and quality of its sunshine. "The climate is the best in the city. If the sun is shining anywhere, it's shining in the Mission."

A multicultural, multiethnic community, it has been described as the most integrated area in San Francisco. The image is cosmopolitan. Approximately 55 percent of the residents are Spanish speaking, and they in turn represent 26 different Latin and Central American countries. There are, in addition to the Whites living in the area, a large number of Filipinos, American Indians, Samoans, and Blacks.

There appears to be some conflict among ethnic groups and within the Latino population. This is especially prevalent in the competition for federal money. One priest notes the divisive effect of what is supposed to be federal support. "The strongest forces can fall apart when federal money is around."

Housing in the Mission consists primarily of converted flats in old victorian homes, apartments in old buildings, and single-family homes. Only 17.5 percent of Mission residents are home owners. This represents the lowest percentage of home owners in the San Francisco neighborhoods and the second lowest of all the sites in this study. Seventy-six percent of the buildings are multi-dwelling buildings. Of these, 24 percent contain seven or more units—the highest percentage of such buildings in the San Francisco sites.

Streets in Mission offer a mixture of contrasting images. One finds a number of streets with deteriorating shabby buildings. "Buildings look dilapidated, dirty and tired. People are poorly dressed and there are many winos hanging out in the doorways." Close by are "long blocks in quiet neighborhoods with beautifully renovated victorian homes." Many windows and doors in Mission houses are covered with grates. Yet there are neighborhoods that reflect the atmosphere of a small town. "People frequently stop to talk to friends." This, in addition to the many restaurants, mom and pop grocery stores, and delicatessens, contributes to the busy congested sidewalks found in parts of the area.

The two public housing projects in Mission are considered neither desirable nor safe. One houses primarily Blacks and is "not a place you'd want to be caught out at night." The other houses mostly Latinos, Filipinos, Samoans, and Asians. This one gives off even "heavier vibes" and "is more of a trouble spot in people's minds."

The Mission shopping area, once known as the miracle mile, is the second biggest in the city. However, the growth of suburban shopping centers, a large redevelopment project in an adjacent area, and the construction of the Bart rapid transit system have contributed to what many merchants consider its serious decline. "Bart had a tremendously negative impact on the Mission. We are still trying to climb back. And when things deteriorate, undesirable businesses move in and try to capitalize on other people's misfortunes."

Although there are still many small reputable businesses as well as some chains in the area, adjacent redevelopment projects forced into the Mission such undesirable businesses as pawn shops, adult bookstores, pornographic theaters, and transient hotels. These, along with the clientele they tend to attract, present a serious threat to the quality of life of the merchants and residents in adjacent neighborhoods.

There are still a number of auto repair shops, metal factories, trucking businesses, and a large savings and loan that offer employment to Mission residents. The departure of a large department store, several furniture companies and breweries, however, have removed from the Mission many of the job opportunities available in the past. This economic decline is reflected in the 14 percent unemployment in the area and the fact that 35 percent of the residents earn under $10,000 (in 1970).

In spite of these dismal figures, one finds enthusiasm and optimism among some residents as they regard the future of their neighborhood. This is especially true of the growing number of young professionals who are buying and renovating houses in the area.

Visitacion Valley, like Mission, is both multicultural and racially integrated. A little more than one quarter of the residents are Black. Visitacion Valley has the highest percentage of home owners among the San Francisco neighborhoods. With the exception of the public housing projects which are predominantly black, the residential areas in Visitacion Valley appear to be ethnically and racially integrated.

There is a variety of housing types within the area. The upper and lower Valley consists of relatively small single-family dwelling units, which constitute 80 percent of the homes in the area. Of these, 67 percent are owner occupied. Many of these are situated on well-kept streets; it is only the bars on the windows and doors that give some indication of the fact that Visitacion Valley has the highest reported crime rate of all the San Francisco sites.

A public housing project and a low-income high rise constitute the bulk of the nonsingle family housing in the area. These are badly maintained and exhibit the usual signs of deterioration—graffiti, boarded up and broken windows, littered streets and sidewalks. Adjacent to the high rise is a town house project that, along with the high rise, had originally been built for a middle-class, professional clientele. The bankruptcy of the developer, however, opened up the high rise to low-income tenants, and this ultimately effected the owners of the town houses who, feeling victimized by their proximity to low-income housing, moved out. The bars and safety devices on these town houses serve as a visible symbol that virtually all the residents have had at least one experience as a burglary victim. Thus, although the original residents of these town houses were the middle class professionals anticipated by the developer who designed the project, their migration out has left a primarily working class population confronting housing values that are stagnating in contrast to the rising values elsewhere in the area.

The residents in the Valley as a whole are mostly working class. There is also a small percentage of middle class professionals and welfare recipients. There is a lower unemployment rate—9 percent— than in the Mission and a lower percentage of people—21 percent— earning less than $10,000. A little less than 10 percent of the residents have college degrees.

The parks and playgrounds in the area constitute problems for the residents. They complain about the "undesirables hanging around the playground" and perceive the park as basically unsafe. It contains a golf course that residents say has been the site of several killings and muggings. It is badly littered and the drives within it are used as drag strips by area youth.

The major commercial strip in the area contains primarily small shops, grocery stores, drug stores, and two larger markets. One of these is known as an area where purse snatchings and muggings are likely to take place. There appear to be no major institutions providing jobs for residents in the area. The one large firm, a lock company, employs few community residents. Nevertheless, its projected departure is expected to adversely affect the commercial establishments nearby.

Perceptions of neighborhood stability are mixed. Although one respondent notes that "people are not committed to staying in the area, there are always two or three houses for sale, most of the kids who have gone to high school and college do not come back," a middle-aged, White resident who has stayed says, "I wouldn't trade living here for any other place in the city."

The most salient fact about Logan is its pervasive and rapid population change. Fifty-five percent of the residents have lived in the area five years or less. Until the mid-1960s, Logan was a predominantly Jewish, White, middle and upper class community. Today it is a low income community with a population that is approximately 50 percent Black. The other 50 percent is comprised of a multiethnic mix of Whites, Korean, Portugese, Filipinos and Hispanics. Although two of the areas within Logan are predominantly Black. the others are both racially and ethnically integrated. Many of the White respondents express the same kind of animosity toward Blacks as is found in South Philadelphia. However, there are others who are actively working to improve relations between the races and who are committed to creating a viable multiracial, multiethnic community.

Most of the housing stock consists of older brick, stone, and wood row houses. The neighborhoods within the community are in variable condition. There are pleasant well-kept areas with tree-lined streets, and then there are areas with narrow streets and large numbers of abandoned and deteriorated housing. Over 73 percent of the housing stock is single-family homes, and 65 percent of the residents are homeowners. Although there are a few scattered apartment buildings, the bulk of the multidwelling houses consists of seven or less units.

There are ample shopping opportunities provided in Logan's two major shopping areas. The area's ethnic heterogeneity is reflected in local businesses; as one resident put it, "you can buy everything you need in Logan." A medical complex, a baking concern, and a district office of the Illinois Bell Telephone Company are the major employment centers in the community. There are several others immediately adjacent to the area.

The individual resources of Logan residents are minimal. Fourteen percent of the residents lack a high school diploma, 16 percent are unemployed, and 35 percent have incomes under $10,000. Although they lack close community ties, which would serve in part to compensate for minimal individual resources in other areas, Logan residents lead a rich organizational life that attempts to foster the community sentiment found more readily in communities with a more stable population.

Perceptions of the neighborhood vary and appear to be somewhat related to the respondents' organizational ties. There is universal agreement that things have changed in Logan. What used to be a very close community where the residents knew each other and felt safe late at night became a heterogeneous neighborhood where many residents felt unsafe. "This used to be a beautiful neighborhood. Now you can't go out of your house without being robbed." Most people, one respondent claimed, live here because they have to. "But it's bad all over."

Respondents with organizational affiliation see a different side of the neighborhood. One block club captain characterizes the area as follows: "This is pretty decent for a mixed neighborhood. Neighbors watch out for each other." A cofounder of the largest community organization in the area notes, "we have a really beautiful community here. There's a beautiful relationship between different groups." And a letter to the editor, which describes Logan as part of the urban renaissance, talks of "quiet serene tree-shaded streets, a sophisticated mix of residents, fantastic shopping and an abundance of parking."

Wicker Park is a small community in the near northwest side of Chicago. The population is predominantly lower working class with a high percentage below the poverty level and a high percentage on public aid. Most of the housing in the area consists of two- and three-story walk-ups.

The exceptions are two public housing high rises for the elderly and an area known as Old Wicker Park, where houses are described as mansions and are being bought and renovated by young professionals. The northeast quadrant of Wicker Park appears to be predominantly Polish and is reasonably well kept. The field worker visiting the area noted few people on the street and only one burned out, boarded up building. This contrasts with the rest of the area where such buildings are most frequently visible. There one also finds a greater ethnic mix with Blacks, Anglos, and Latinos visible on the same blocks. Housing also is mixed, with buildings ranging from *excellent* to *terrible*. Many of the badly maintained buildings are owned by slum lords who live outside the community. Vacant lots dot the area. Many of these are previously contained housing destroyed by arson and are littered with garbage and weeds.

Although most residential areas are laced with small industrial sites, Milwaukee Avenue provides a focus for the community's retail business. There one finds clothing and furniture stores, as well as restaurants, bars, drug stores, and a theater. Wicker Park has no major employers. Banks, offices, and light industry are often interspersed with residential neighborhoods. Many of the businesses are small, family operated storefronts that keep their doors locked during working hours.

The population has changed greatly since the early 1960s when it was primarily a Polish neighborhood. The neighborhood surveys indicate that 22 percent of the population is Puerto Rican, although the field worker was given estimates ranging from 40 to 60 percent. Mexicans make up 8 percent of the population, and Blacks 14 percent. The tight job market faced by the more recent immigrants is reflected in a 14 percent unemployment rate. Almost 40 percent of the residents have no high school diploma, and a little under 6 percent are college graduates.

Although a minority of the respondents are optimistic about the area and offered positive assessments, the majority expressed extremely negative images. A priest active in the Northwest Community Organization optimistically commented that he found a "sense of community. People who live here like living here and plan to stay. People are learning to live with each other." This assessment finds some support in the fact that 55 percent of the people surveyed in the area expected to live in the neighborhood two years from now. A Czech realtor, interested in attracting White clientele, described the community as pretty stable.

The other respondents, however, present a different picture. An elderly public housing tenant estimated that the neighborhood was about 85 percent unsafe. All her acquaintances had had experiences with purse snatchers.

Younger people find the community reasonably safe in the daytime when "everyone knows where they are supposed to be," but much less safe at night; "the gangs come out and there's a lot going on." The quality of life in the neighborhood for her was neatly summed up by a 12 year old parochial student who said, "it feels just terrible to be walking alone around four o'clock in the afternoon."

Conclusion

Although many of the differences in our research sites reflect the socioeconomic status and the racial composition of their populations, there are others that are less easily categorized. The neighborhoods vary in their position on the neighborhood change cycle. Some are perceived as improving, others are deteriorating, and still others are seen as stable. And they vary in the responses these changes evoke. These depend as much on the socioeconomic status and resources of the residents as on any objective definition of improvement or deterioration. Low-income residents who cannot afford the rents in "improving" neighborhoods clearly cannot interpret this as a beneficial change.

Furthermore, neighborhoods vary in the images they evoke and in the sentiments they provoke. These responses we believe are most closely related to feelings of security and fear and are most readily understood by a careful examination of those forces in the neighborhood that cause concern and those that provide a measure of comfort and control.

4

Fear of Crime in the Neighborhoods

Data and Methodology

The theoretical framework that guides our analysis requires that we be equally sensitive to community and individual characteristics. We have used survey questions that focus on individual attitudes and behavior. But we will use that data to help delineate neighborhood context. For example, we will not discuss the differences between individuals who are and are not afraid. Rather, we will compare neighborhoods where a large percentage of the residents are afraid with those neighborhoods where this is not the case. This approach falls in the tradition of the Chicago School's analysis of crime, which was begun by Shaw and McKay in the ecological study of Chicago community areas, *Delinquency Areas* (1929). In this study, they characterized the Chicago neighborhoods according to the level of "official" delinquency committed by residents in the area. This was followed by the study of the life history of one delinquent in *The Jackroller* (Shaw 1930). In using these two approaches to understand criminal behavior, Shaw and McKay wanted not only to show the relationship between the characteristics of communities and the amount of delinquency they produce, but also how the community served as a context which influenced the activities of those living within it. The problem, then and today, is to address the influence of context on individual behavior and attitudes without committing the ecological fallacy.

We have kept this problem in mind as we compare the attitudes and behavior of individuals living in areas characterized by differences in the percentage of people reporting fear of crime. We will show that the individual characteristics usually associated with variations in fear cannot account for all of the differences exhibited in our study sites.

We wish to acknowledge the contribution of Ron Szoc to the statistical analyses presented in this section.

And we will argue that contextual variables will provide insight and explanations for the differences we have found.

Our data was collected as part of the general data gathering activity of the Reactions to Crime Project at the Center for Urban Affairs at Northwestern University. This was a long-term research endeavor funded by the National Institute of Law Enforcement and Criminal Justice and the Law Enforcement Assistance Administration to assess the impact of crime on city dwellers. Data collection techniques included a random digit dialing telephone survey, fifteen months of field work in each community, a content analysis of the metropolitan newspapers in each of the three cities, and the use of archival data (e.g., crime data, census data, and so forth). The multimethod strategy employed in the project provided a unique opportunity in social science research to combine the benefits of survey research, which provides breadth of information with the depth of understanding derived from the qualitative research of the field work.

The following discussion of the field work is based on the more detailed account found in the "Methodological Overview of the Reactions to Crime Project," edited by Michael Maxfield and Albert Hunter. Because we were investigating a topic about which little was known, we utilized the participant observation methods in the initial phase of the research. The strength of this method lies in the detailed knowledge provided about individuals and their social settings. The weaknesses are related to problems of validity and reliability of observations.

Teams of field workers and a field director operated in each city from April 1976 through August 1977. The city directors maintained contact with project headquarters at Northwestern to coordinate activities at the field sites. Research teams in each city employed a variety of methods to observe and collect information about each of these neighborhoods. Interview methods ranged from casual conversations with acquaintances on the street to more formal interviews with systematically selected respondents and community leaders. Special efforts were made to seek out a wide range of community leaders and other influential residents. Field workers also attended meetings of local organizations and collected a series of unobtrusive indicators relating to the physical and social characteristics of the neighborhoods, demographic changes, and patterns of street use.

Although the field work did not concentrate on focused interviews or standard lists of information to be obtained from each neighborhood, some formal interviews and uniform data gathering guidelines were used. In addition, at about the midpoint in the participant observation phase of the field work, field manuals and various questionnaires were developed by the central project staff to obtain some similar types of information about crime issues and group activities in the neighborhood. This research produced over 8,000 pages of field notes that were coded and prepared for analysis. The comparative analysis in the discussion that follows is based on a detailed coding scheme that allowed the analysts of the field notes to impose *post hoc* a comparative structure on the details provided in the individual field note observations.

The field data not only helped us to identify those aspects of the local environment that generated concern among local residents, but they also forced some reassessment of the conceptual categories with which we began our research. For example, we assumed that when we discussed fear-producing criminal events, the concern would be with index crimes such as robbery, burglary, assault, and so forth. However, discussions with area residents repeatedly revealed that fear was frequently triggered by an abundance of abandoned housing in a neighborhood, groups of teenagers hanging around, evidence that there was drug use and abuse, and varying signs of vandalism.

Because the field work was conducted the year before the telephone survey was administered, we were able to incorporate questions drawn from the insights derived from the field data. The survey was administered to 5,200 respondents in the ten localities and to an independent sample of 540 respondents in each city. Survey questions dealt with victimization experiences, knowledge about the victimization of others, where that knowledge was acquired (media, personal contact), perceptions about crime and crime related activities, concerns about neighborhood problems, and individual and collectively organized responses to perceived dangers in the neighborhood.

In the discussion that follows, we use the survey data to show how the several places, their parts, and their connections appear to affect community residents. And we use the comparative case study approach to look across communities to determine whether the contextual forces that we have hypothesized to be operating are in fact associated with the fear levels we have found.

Fear of Crime in Ten Communities

We have used one item in the telephone survey to measure fear of crime.

> How safe do you feel, or would you feel, being out alone in your neighborhood *at night*—very safe, somewhat safe, somewhat unsafe or very unsafe?

This item is a slight modification of the item most generally used in previous surveys to measure fear of crime (Cook and Cook 1975). Figure 1 shows the distribution of fear levels in the ten neighborhoods as well as the city-wide means. The ten communities range from a high of 54 percent to a low of 24 percent of the residents reporting fear. Interestingly enough, there is almost no difference in the fear levels of the city-wide samples. Approximately 30 percent of the residents in each city reported fear of crime. The major differences are to be found between the neighborhoods, and it is these that we must consider as we seek to identify the variables that will account for them. In the remainder of this chapter, we will look at those variables traditionally associated with fear of crime: the criminal environment in each of the communities and the demographic characteristics of the individuals living within them.

The Criminal Environment

An initial step in searching for explanations for these differences must consider the variation in criminal activity and victimization experiences in each of these neighborhoods. Perceived increases in crime are among the clearest indicators of social disorder in an area and one of the most potent stimulants to fear. The strong relationship between victimization experiences or even knowing about a local crime victim and fear has been well documented (Skogan, 1980). However, measuring the impact of crime on behavior and attitudes poses several problems. Crime rates and victimization surveys tell us about the prevalance of crime in an area, but do not indicate its salience to the inhabitants. Measures of awareness and concern, on the other hand, tell us little about the realities on which these attitudes are based. Recognizing that all of our measures are somewhat imperfect, we combined them to provide an assessment of what we call the criminal environment in each of the neighborhoods. We used the survey items noted below to characterize the criminal environment in each of the neighborhoods.

1. Reported crime rates for each neighborhood
2. Concern about crime as a neighborhood problem
3. Knowing a local victim—vicarious victimization

In the following section we describe the indicators of victimization and the manner in which each of them was operationalized.

FIGURE 1
Fear of Crime*
(Percent feel unsafe in neighborhood at night)

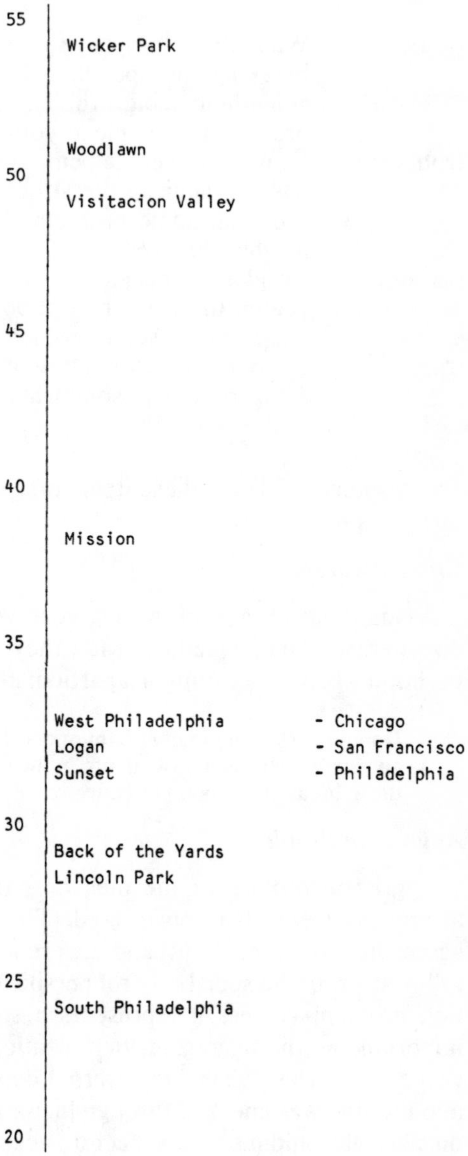

```
55 ─┤
     │    Wicker Park
     │
     │
     │    Woodlawn
50 ─┤
     │    Visitacion Valley
     │
     │
45 ─┤
     │
     │
     │
40 ─┤
     │    Mission
     │
     │
35 ─┤
     │
     │    West Philadelphia      - Chicago
     │    Logan                  - San Francisco
     │    Sunset                 - Philadelphia
30 ─┤
     │    Back of the Yards
     │    Lincoln Park
     │
25 ─┤
     │    South Philadelphia
     │
     │
20 ─┤
```

* Missing values have
been excluded from
analysis

Concern About Victimization

The survey respondents were asked whether four types of crime were neighborhood problems. The exact wording of the questions was as follows:

(burglary)   What about burglary for the neighborhood in general? Is breaking into people's homes or sneaking in to steal something a big problem, some problem, or almost no problem for people in your neighborhood?

(robbery)   How about people being robbed or having their purses or wallets taken in the street? Would you say this is a big problem, some problem, or almost no problem in your neighborhood?

(assault)   Besides robbery, how about people being attacked or beaten up in your neighborhood by strangers? Is this a big problem, some problem, or almost no problem?

(rape)   In your neighborhood, would you say sexual assaults are a big problem, somewhat of a problem, or almost no problem at all?

The response scale for these items ranged from *1* (almost no problem) to *3* (big problem).

Crime Awareness

As another indicator of the degree to which residents perceive social disorder, we asked whether or not they knew someone in their neighborhood who was a victim of a particular crime. Specifically, we asked:

Do you personally know of anyone, other than yourself, whose home or apartment has been broken into in the past year or so? (if yes) Did any of these break-ins happen in your present neighborhood?

Aggregate Profiles

Aggregate profiles of the measures of crime concerns and crime awareness were also constructed. The rationale for developing the aggregate concern about and awareness of crime scales were as follows: From the social control perspective, any individual victimization problem—unless it represents a sudden crime wave—is not as important as the aggregate victimization problem across all serious crime categories. Thus, the internal consistency of all four concerns about crime was checked through factor analysis (all four items loaded on a single unidimensional factor, accounting for 51 percent of the variance) and calculation of Cronbach's alpha coefficient on the pooled city-wide samples. All four items were moderately correlated with the sum of the other three and together formed a scale with an alpha coefficient of .674. The position of a neighborhood on the concern about victimization scale was determined by the percentage of responses that were "big problems" for the four crimes.

The awareness of crime variable represents aggregation of four counter variables, representing whether a respondent knew a local victim of each type of crime. Each of the counter variables for robbery, attack, and rape could range in value from 0 to 3, depending on how many local victims a respondent knew for each crime. Because the knowledge of burglary victims was asked in a different way, the counter variable for burglary could assume either a 0 or 1. The awareness of crime variable was then computed by counting how many of these crime-specific counter variables had nonzero values.

In sum, we have combined resident attitudes and experiences in the conceptualization of the criminal environment in the neighborhoods. The measure of concern about crime victimization as a neighborhood problem permits us to assess the extent of residents' concern about specific crimes without necessarily including a personal dimension (i.e., "a big problem for me"). It can be assumed that this reflects the integration of information and attitudes from neighbors and from local media coverage. The indirect experience with victimization supplements the data on the reported crime rate for each area. We believe this adds an important dimension for the following reasons: (1) few people are aware of reported crime statistics; (2) it is unclear how the magnitude of a reported crime statistic (e.g., a burglary rate of 35 per 1000) effects any person's attitude; and (3) crime statistics are typically not made known at a neighborhood level. We look next at the criminal environment in the ten neighborhoods.

Figure 2 represents the crime rate for each of the ten neighborhoods, the percentage of residents who know a crime victim, the percentage who consider crime to be a big problem, and the percentage who are afraid to walk in their neighborhoods at night. The crime rate and concern measures represent profiles for four combined crimes—burglary, assault, robbery and rape. Because the rankings on the crime rate measures are somewhat skewed by intercity variations in reporting procedures, we have included the mean crime rate for each of the cities. Four of the neighborhoods—Woodlawn, Wicker Park, Lincoln Park, and Visitacion Valley—are fifteen or more units above their city's mean. Four other neighborhoods—Mission, Back of the Yards, West Philadelphia, and Logan—are within three units of their city's mean, and two—South Philadelphia and Sunset—fall well below.

FIGURE 2
Crime Rates, Crime Concerns and Fear

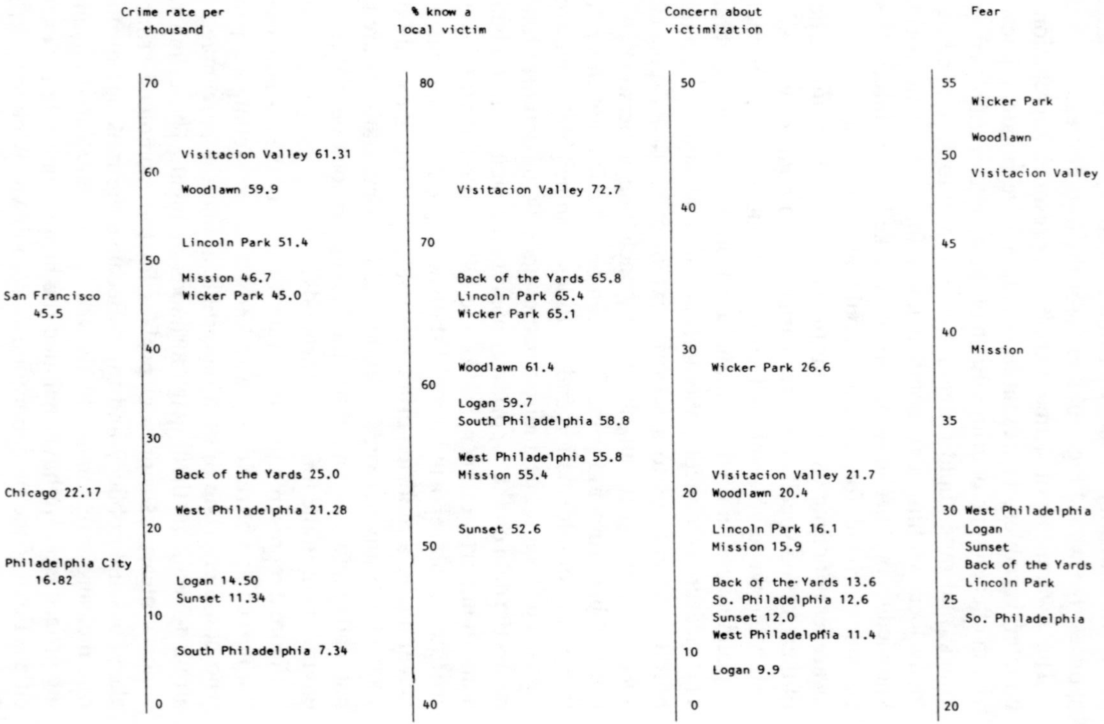

Crime rate per thousand	% know a local victim	Concern about victimization	Fear
			55 — Wicker Park
			Woodlawn
			50 — Visitacion Valley
70 —			
			45 —
Visitacion Valley 61.31			
60 — Woodlawn 59.9			40 — Mission
Lincoln Park 51.4			35 —
50 — Mission 46.7			
Wicker Park 45.0			30 — West Philadelphia
San Francisco 45.5			Logan
40 —			Sunset
			Back of the Yards
			25 — Lincoln Park
Back of the Yards 25.0			So. Philadelphia
30 —			
West Philadelphia 21.28			20 —
Chicago 22.17			
20 —			
Logan 14.50			
Sunset 11.34			
Philadelphia City 16.82			
10 —			
South Philadelphia 7.34			
0 —			

% know a local victim
80 —
Visitacion Valley 72.7
70 — Back of the Yards 65.8
Lincoln Park 65.4
Wicker Park 65.1
60 — Woodlawn 61.4
Logan 59.7
South Philadelphia 58.8
West Philadelphia 55.8
Mission 55.4
50 — Sunset 52.6
40 —

Concern about victimization
50 —
40 —
30 — Wicker Park 26.6
Visitacion Valley 21.7
20 — Woodlawn 20.4
Lincoln Park 16.1
Mission 15.9
Back of the Yards 13.6
So. Philadelphia 12.6
Sunset 12.0
West Philadelphia 11.4
10 — Logan 9.9
0 —

A comparison of the neighborhoods on the crime rate and fear measures indicates anomalies similar to those found in the previous fear of crime analyses discussed earlier. Wicker Park, which ranks fifth among the neighborhoods in crime rates, is at the top of the list in the percentage of residents expressing fear of crime. And Lincoln Park, with one of the higher crime rates in the group, moves way down on the fear measure into a group of neighborhoods with considerably less crime.

These differences are consistent with the variations in levels of concern illustrated in Figure 3. Here we see that Wicker Park, with a crime rate lower than four of the other neighborhoods, ranks first in the measure of concern. In Lincoln Park, on the other hand, we see a relatively high crime rate combined with a lower ranking on the concern measure. And in Sunset and South Philadelphia, larger percentages of residents exhibit concern than in the two other Philadelphia neighborhoods that have higher crime rates.

Concern about crime may vary because of differences in crime rates or because of differences in neighborhood communication patterns of transmitting information about crime. This is evident in Figure 2, which shows Back of the Yards with a lower crime rate, but exhibiting higher levels of awareness than a number of neighborhoods with more crime and less awareness. The fact that the percentage of residents knowing local victims exceeds those expressing concern about crime indicates that what we have called indirect victimization is not automatically translated into concern. And the fact that the percentage expressing fear exceeds those expressing concern suggests that crime alone cannot account for the fear reported in most neighborhoods.

Furthermore, Wicker Park's position on the fear measure indicates that there may well be fear engendering conditions there that are not at work in the other high crime neighborhoods. And Lincoln Park's position in a cluster of neighborhoods with considerably lower crime rates suggests there may be conditions in Lincoln Park that foster feelings of security and counteract those fostering fear.

This lack of congruence between the crime rate, the indirect victimization experiences, the concern about crime, and the fear of crime in our research sites clearly suggests that we need to look further in seeking to understand the conditions that generate fear of crime among urban residents. However, before examining the variables associated with neighborhood context, we need to determine if the differences that we have found are not due to variations in the demographic characteristics of the neighborhood residents. We examine next those most frequently associated with fear of crime.

FIGURE 3
Concern About Victimization

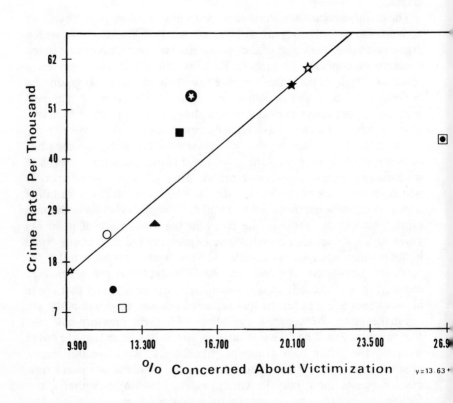

Individual Characteristics and Fear of Crime

Age, sex, and race have been used by dozens of scholars to explain variations in the fear of individuals. If the differences between communities can be accounted for by the characteristics of their residents, there may be no need to introduce contextual factors. If, however, we find support for the importance of contextual variables we can proceed to a more complete investigation of the community contexts.

Table 2 reports a regression analysis of fear of crime with individual characteristics. The dependent variable was a seven-score consolidation of three separate variables: (1) fear of crime during the day, (2) fear of crime during the night, and (3) risk for personal crime. The risk for personal crime measure was a consolidation of the feeling that an individual might be robbed or assaulted.

To investigate the internal consistency of these items, Cronbach's alpha coefficient was calculated. Together the three variables form a scale with an alpha coefficient of .67. Given this moderate consistency and the general face validity of the two items, the fear variable has adequate construct validity to support its use. The individual characteristics variables in the left-hand column represent straightforward items from the random-digit-dialing telephone survey. The assessment of neighborhood conditions variables are divided into two clusters, major crimes and incivilities. Both are formed from the gain of standardized responses to them in the same survey, and variable clusters are more fully described in the next chapter. At this point it is sufficient to say that both clusters tap "how big a problem" victimizations (robbery, burglary, rape, and assault) are and "how big a problem" incivilities (adolescent loitering, abandoned buildings, drug use, and vandalism) are in the respondents' communities. The personal linkage variables following Riger and Lavrakas (1981) tap different types of social integration in the neighborhoods. Table 3 shows how those factors were developed from the telephone survey by Riger and Lavrakas. An internal consistency check was performed on each set of three items that defined the two factors. The three items that load in Factor 1 can be combined to form an additive index with an alpha coefficient of .59. The three items that load in Factor 2 can be combined to form an additive index with an internal consistency of .56 (Riger and Lavrakas 1981). All these variables reflect the major independent and intervening variables proposed in the social control perspective. By testing them at the individual level, we can assess the viability of the perspective and the importance of contextual variables.

As Table 2 indicates, all the variables, with the exception of the

residential linkage variable, are significant at the .01 level. It is important to note the strength of the zero-order correlations in the right-hand
column, particularly the assessment of neighborhood conditions. The
fact that these correlations are the most robust in the analysis gives us
a strong indication that context plays an important role in generating
fear. Our next step, taken in Table 4, is to determine whether we can

TABLE 2
Regression Analysis of Fear of Crime:
Individual Characteristics

Variables	Standardized Regression Coefficient (Beta)	Significance	Zero-order Correlation
Individual Characteristics			
Sex (female)	.23	.01	.29
Elderly	.11	.01	.14
Race (Black)	.05	.01	.04
Education	-.07	.01	-.13
Assessments of Neighborhood Conditions			
Major crimes	.38	.01	.50
Incivilities	.17	.01	.36
Personal Linkages to Community			
Social (Bonded)	-.12	.01	-.16
Residential (Rooted)	.01	.64	-.01

R^2 = .37
N = 1737

TABLE 3
Oblique Factor Matrix for Neighborhood Integration Items

Item	Factor loading[a]	
	Factor 1-Rooted	Factor 2-Bonded
1. In general is it pretty easy or pretty difficult for you to tell a stranger in your neighborhood from someone who lives there?	-.11	.76
2. Would you say that you really feel a part of your neighborhood or do you think of it more as just a place to live?	.19	.35
3. How about kids in your immediate neighborhood? How many of them do you know by name: all of them, some, hardly any, or none of them?	.12	.49
4. How many years have you personally lived in your present neighborhood?	.47	.02
5. Do you own your home or do you rent it?	.66	.02
6. Do you expect to be living in this neighborhood 2 years from now?	.49	-.02
% total variance	37.60	16.80
Eigenvalues	2.26	1.01

[a]Weighted n = 1,158.

Source: Riger and Lavrakas, 1981

TABLE 4
Regression Analysis of Fear of Crime:
Individual and Neighborhood Components

Variable Cluster	Direct R^2 with Fear[a]	Incremental Addition to R^2 with Fear[b]	Significance of Incremental Effect[c]	
			F	SigF.
Individual Characteristics				
(Four individual measures)	10.5	7.8	53.87	.01
Assessments of Conditions				
(Two multiple-component measures)	27.3	19.2	265.00	.01
Personal Linkages to Community				
(Two multiple-component measures)	3.0	1.1	16.95	.01
Neighborhood of Residence				
(Dichotomous predictors)	5.6	1.4	3.96	.01

[a] Multiple R^2 using only variables in cluster

[b] Addition to multiple R^2 controlling for all other clusters

[c] Calculated following Theib, 1971, p. 138-140.

increase the amount of variance explained when we add neighborhood of residence to the regressions analysis. This is important for it gives further testimony to the importance of community context in explaining the fear of individuals. In Table 3 we cluster the variables analyzed in Table 2 and add neighborhood of residence to the regression. Again, all the variable clusters are significant at the .01 level, including neighborhood of residence. Notice in particular how robust the assessment of conditions is *and* the significance of neighborhood of residence in the same regression equation. Thus, we have evidence that both place of residence and assessments of the place are significantly related to fear of crime after individual level variables are accounted for. These findings indicate that a contextual analysis is appropriate, and fear of crime is related not only to individual but also to contextual variables.

In the following two chapters, we examine the relevant contexts. We look first at neighborhood change and social disorganization in Chapter 5. Then we investigate the strategies and resources residents use to deal with and limit the perceived threats to the integrity of their communities in Chapter 6.

5

Social Disorganization and Neighborhood Change

All neighborhoods are characterized by an ambiance that provides cues both to the residents and to outsiders about what kind of neighborhood this might be. These cues, however, are differentially perceived, not only in accordance with one's status as an insider or outsider, but also in accordance with one's position in the neighborhood itself. Perceptions are frequently colored by age, race, socioeconomic or other characteristics that determine one's status as a member of a minority or dominant group in a given area.

In this chapter we discuss those conditions that have been defined by the neighborhood residents as problems and as indications that things are not going well. We call these indicators of incivility and describe the way that they were operationally defined below. These indicators were all initially defined as neighborhood problems in the field research and do not reflect ideas or categories imposed by the researchers. Some of these concerns were subsequently incorporated as items in the telephone survey. Others are derived from a content analysis of the field notes.

Indicators of Incivility

The indicators of incivility described below represent neighborhood conditions that produce anxiety among neighborhood residents. Such fear generating situations involve either threatening physical conditions, changes in the environment, or improper conduct on the part of the individuals, which may or may not be classified as criminal. Since some of the indicators are drawn from the survey and others from a content analysis of the field notes, they range from very quantitative to qualitative in nature.

Following is a list of the indicators:

1. Concern about various signs of "incivility" as a neighborhood problem

2. Descriptions of neighborhood physical decay
3. Perceptions on the part of the neighborhood activists that the neighborhood is being inadequately served by city machinery
4. Presence and degree of ethnic conflict
5. Introduction of undesirable businesses in commercial areas in the neighborhood

Indicator *1* is derived from the telephone survey. Indicators *2* through *5*, drawn from the content analysis of the field notes, are essentially impressions of recurring themes heard from neighborhood residents and key persons in various neighborhood groups. The following section discusses the exact manner in which the incivility indicators were operationally defined.

Concern About Neighborhood Signs of Incivility

In order to assess the levels of concern that residents felt about various signs of neighborhood disorganization, the following questions were asked of the respondents in the telephone survey sample:

• Groups of teenagers hanging out on the streets. Is this a big problem, some problem, or almost no problem in your neighborhood?
• Buildings or storefronts sitting abandoned or burned out. Is this a big problem, some problem, or almost no problem in your neighborhood?
• People using illegal drugs in the neighborhood. Is this a big problem, some problem, or almost no problem?
• Vandalism, like kids breaking windows or writing on walls or things like that. How much of a problem is this?

These particular indicators were developed in conjunction with the field work. When field workers asked neighborhood residents what the nature of the local crime problem was, residents typically included descriptions of teenage loitering or drug activity as neighborhood ills. Inclusion of these items in the survey permitted us to systematically assess the extent to which the neighorhoods vary with respect to residents' perceptions of noncriminal indicators of social disorder.

Aggregate profiles of these measures of incivility were also constructed. It was hypothesized that all four signs of incivility (loitering youth, drugs, vandalism, and abandoned buildings) would define a construct representing the extent to which there was a perceived problem with social disorganization in the neighborhood. Accordingly, a factor analysis of the four indicators was performed on the pooled city-wide samples. All the items were undimensional and significantly intercorrelated. The internal consistence of these items formed a scale with an alpha of .755. The position of a neighborhood on the concern about the social order scale was determined by the percentage of responses that were "big problems" for any of the four questionnaire items. The remaining indicators were culled from the field notes and represent either expressed concerns or conditions in the the neighborhood that are interpreted as threatening. These indicators include the following:

- *The presence or arrival of undesirable businesses*
  Whether or not a business is seen as undesirable is a subjective assessment. But, businesses so categorized are unwanted typically because of the type of clientele they are perceived to attract, regardless of whether or not they actually do. The presence or arrival of such businesses may symbolize the lack of control residents potentially have over their environments.
- *Inadequately served by city services*
  This indicator permits us to assess how important and how locally powerful a community is with respect to its demands for municipal attention; another aspect of its local controlling ability.
- *Description of neighborhood physical decay*
  This indicator permits us to assess the extent to which a neighborhood's residents have control of their community's land and its uses. It will be seen in the following section that in some areas, the presence or absence of physical decay is directly related to the municipal political power that a community can marshall.
- *Presence and degree of ethnic conflict*
  Ethnic conflict is another indicator of the degree of control residents have over their neighborhood. Apart from racism, this indicator also can be used to infer the degree of competition residents experience in their neighborhood for community resources, and the type of dispute settlement that the area's residents engage in to solve difficulties.

With all the indicators described above, of course, there exist varying degrees of subjectivity. While the questions on the survey directly ask for subjective assessment, the other indicators involve an opinion on the part of the field workers or on our part in interpreting the field notes. Nevertheless, we feel that the social control perspective demands a careful scrutiny of all the available sources of data; it requires a multimethod, multiindicator approach. In this way, we develop a broader base to theorize from and, at the same time, allow the richness of the experiences and attitudes of the residents to present themselves. We look next at those indicators of incivility in the ten neighborhoods that reflect the degree of social disorganization perceived by area residents.

Incivility In the Ten Neighborhoods

Of the four incivility indicators tapped in the telephone survey, two—illegal use of drugs and vandalism—are illegal behaviors tangentially associated with more serious crimes. The other two—teenagers hanging around and abandoned buildings—serve as cues indicating to neighborhood residents that the area is changing in unwelcome ways. Teenagers hanging around constitute a particular threat in transitional areas where age and ethnic differences combine to create tension in the neighborhood. White, elderly Polish women tend to be fearful about all teenagers. But they are even more fearful when those teenagers are Black or Hispanic.

Figure 4 presents the percentage of residents in the ten neighborhoods exhibiting concern about these four problems. There we note that a large percentage of residents in Wicker Park express concern about every one of these problems. At the same time, Sunset is characterized by the lowest levels of concern. Significant percentages of residents in South Philadelphia, Back of the Yards, and Mission join those in the high crime areas in their concern about teens and teen-related activities. In South Philadelphia and Mission, the major problem is drug use. In Back of the Yards, it is vandalism. Physical maintenance problems reflected in the abandoned buildings chart appear to be most serious in Woodlawn and Wicker Park, but present minimal concern to the residents in the San Francisco neighborhoods and in Lincoln Park.

The conditions generating these concerns as well as those untapped in our survey are more fully described by our field data. Residents' descriptions of neighborhood conditions in Wicker Park make its position at the top of the incivility concern measures readily understandable. Concern about abandoned buildings reflects the generally deteriorating condition in the neighborhood. Neighborhood bars attract an unsavory clientele that spills out into the streets, and although there are islands of well-kept homes where the older, White, Polish families reside and where young professionals are renovating old "mansions," the major sections of the neighborhood are generally viewed as deteriorating and dangerous.

Concerns about teens and drugs reflect the area's gang problem. Although several sites in this study have experienced such difficulties in the past, Wicker Park is the only neighborhood that was confronting serious disruptions by youth gangs during the study period. Violence is

FIGURE 4
Concern about Incivility

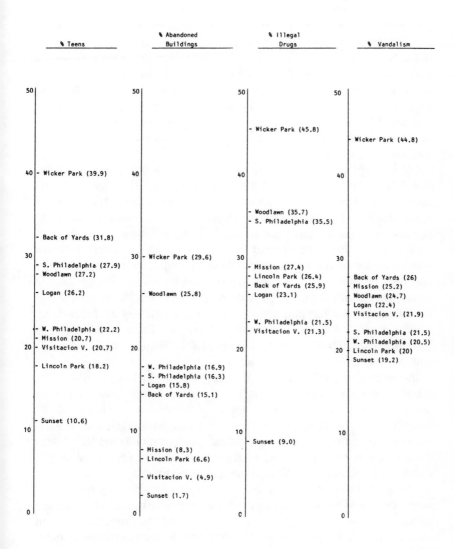

common in the schools. A fight between a Latino and a Black elementary school girl and an assault by a Black student on a White elementary principal are among incidents reported in the field data reflecting the tension and hostility confronted by young people on a daily basis.

Crime, as we have noted, is a serious problem for residents in Wicker Park. But our survey questions did not tap the most frightening crime of all. Suspected arson fires were frequent occurrences in the area and played a critical role in generating unease among neighborhood residents. A sit-in was staged in the mayor's office after a particularly devastating fire killed seven people and graphically illustrated the danger involved when Anglo firemen are unable to communicate with Latino victims. A city arson task force was subsequently created, but it served more as a symbolic response and offered little help to residents who felt compelled to take turns staying up at night to watch for arsonists.

Other problems discussed by residents indicated a number of additional incivility indicators undetected in the telephone survey. The ethnic mix in Wicker Park appears to generate a fairly high level of ethnic conflict. Negative stereotypes are pervasive. The elderly, White population is particularly hostile to the Puerto Ricans, who are perceived to be dirty, irresponsible transients with no interests in or commitments to the community. White parents are resentful of the special attention given Latinos in the school's bilingual program and insist that Spanish-speaking residents are unwilling to participate in school affairs. Latino parents, on the other hand, feel excluded from events where no Spanish translations are provided. The conflict is further aggravated by the age gap between the White, elderly residents and the younger Latinos and Blacks.

Intraminority conflict is also evident. Puerto Ricans feel that they are the most disadvantaged and badly served group in the neighborhood. Minority programs, they argue, are geared to the needs of the Black population. Mexicans are also seen as more advantaged. In fact, intraLatino conflict is almost as common as interracial conflict. Puerto Ricans resent the Mexicans, and neither group is very fond of the Cubans who are more socioeconomically advantaged.

Residents in Wicker Park confront many barriers as they try to deal with the physical deterioration of the neighborhood. They report difficulty in forcing the many absentee slumlords to properly maintain their buildings. They claim that they are unable to ascertain ownership of the abandoned, dilapidated buildings and vacant lots in their area. And they report that they are unable to obtain mortgage money to improve their homes.

Wicker Park residents have particularly poor relationships with both the political establishment and the police. The police are seen as ineffective, uninterested, corrupt, and prejudiced against the Latino residents. Police brutality is a major issue in the neighborhood. Police are seen as racists who do not respond quickly to Spanish-speaking callers. There are complaints about the inadequate representation of Latinos on the police force and the dissatisfaction with Latinos who are on the force. Latino policemen are frequently paired with White policemen. Thus, they feel pressured to treat Lations harshly in order to show "that they can be tough on their own."

Police, on the other hand, have an equally dismal view of the population they serve. They complain about lack of citizen cooperation. Latino policemen feel pressured and used by their own people. "I would like to help them out with some of their problems, but they don't deserve it. They use you and then screw you."

Relations between the dominant community organization, the Northwest Community Organization (NCO), and the police are poor. A police neighbohood relations officer sees the organization leaders as "opportunists who stir people up against the police and circulate rumors that the politicians, realtors, and landlords are behind the arson in the area. They are traitors to Chicago . . . . They demand instead of requesting respectfully."

NCO members, on the other hand, feel betrayed by the politicians and city agencies. Many believe that real estate speculators and politicians are connected with the arson in the area, which is seen as a mechanism for clearing the land to make room for the higher priced housing they wish to construct.

There is some evidence to support this sentiment. The former alderman of the ward was convicted of fraud in land speculation deals in the area. And, repeatedly, public officials invited to organization meetings in the community did not attend and frequently failed even to respond to the invitation. The neighborhood development plans drawn up by the two groups in the area did not receive the support of the two aldermen representing this community.

The difficulties confronted by Woodlawn residents are in many ways similar to those in Wicker Park. Physical maintenance problems are severe. The majority of the buildings in the area are multiple-unit apartment buildings, usually run-down and deteriorated in appearance. Many of them are owned by absentee landlords who find it economically unfeasible to maintain them adequately. Often tenants are unable to ascertain their landlord's identity and, thus, cannot confront the person or persons responsible for the conditions in which they live.

Many of the more threatening situations currently endemic in Wicker Park are part of Woodlawn's history. In the early 1970s, gang violence was a serious problem and arson had reached epidemic proportions. However, gangs have become less evident and arson is no longer a problem because, as one fire captain put it, "there's nothing left to burn."

However, antisocial activities most frequently associated with gangs and teens, such as drug use, drug selling, and vandalism, continue to be major concerns. Most of the crime in the area is attributed to the heavy drug use and frequent addiction found among the residents.

One finds in Woodlawn many of the negative perceptions of the police and political establishments exhibited by the activists in Wicker Park, but there is a qualitative difference. While the majority of the respondents in Woodlawn reflect a weariness about the police, there is not the same intense hostility and feeling that the police are ineffective and cannot do much about residents' problems as one finds in Wicker Park. There is less discussion in Woodlawn about police harassment and brutality and more talk about the constraints policemen face in their efforts to control crime in the neighborhood.

Woodlawn activists also find reason to complain about the quality of the services the city provides for them. The education offered in the public schools has been defined as largely irrelevant to the needs of the youth of the community. In addition, control of the community is seen as problematic. One finds in Woodlawn some of the same concern about the establishment and its plan for the area that is so prevalent in Wicker Park. Much of the hostility is directed at the University of Chicago, which some feel will determine the future of the area. There are the same difficulties in identifying owners of abandoned buildings and vacant lots and the same suspicions about the interests of the owners. As one respondent put it, "the real criminals are the real estate interests."

Although the field data suggest that the incivility indicators in Wicker Park and Woodlawn are similar, there are interesting differences in levels of concern expressed by the residents. Whereas Wicker Park ranks first in concern about teenagers and vandalism, Woodlawn ranks fourth, with approximately half the percentage of residents in Woodlawn as in Wicker Park expressing such concern. And although Woodlawn ranks second to Wicker Park in the percentage of residents expressing concern about drugs and abandoned buildings, there is a difference of eleven percentage points between the two neighborhoods on the first issue and approximately four percentage points difference on the second.

These differences in concern levels might well be accounted for by the racial homogeneity in Woodlawn. There is evidence (Stinchcombe 1978) that proximity to racially diverse groups increases levels of fear. It is possible that levels of concern about the basically similar conditions are higher in Wicker Park because of the intrusion of ethnically diverse groups into the area.

Although South Philadelphia differs from Wicker Park and Woodlawn along most dimensions, its residents share with the other two neighborhoods the highest drug concern levels. Field interviews reflect perceptions of widespread drug use and the devastating consequences for the area. The concerns expressed are multifaceted. There is first the physical problem of pervasive drug addiction. One respondent described a three-block area housing twenty-five hard core heroin addicts. Second, there is the danger posed by pushers in the neighborhood selling drugs to young children who are not yet addicted. And finally, there are all the drug-related crime problems. The president of one neighborhood group created specifically to deal with problems generated by drug use noted that in his area a hundred people a week are robbed or mugged. Although the figures might be exaggerated, the connection is clear. Drug addicts are perceived as needing money to support their habit and willing to do whatever is necessary to get it. Several parents reported being robbed, and in some instances beaten, by their own drug-addicted children.

The field notes indicate that there is more tolerance in South Philadelphia for teenagers hanging around than one finds in most neighborhoods. Thus, the fact that South Philadelphia ranks third on the survey measure of concern about teenagers suggests that this issue for South Philadelphians is confounded by their concern about drugs.

The field note descriptions of the other two Philadelphia neighborhoods, West Philadelphia and Logan, are similar in many ways to those of Woodlawn and Wicker Park. The residents in both complain about abandoned housing, vacant lots and deteriorating commercial districts. Like Woodlawn, both neighborhoods experienced disruptive gang violence in the early 1970s, which has since abated. The residents in Logan, like those in Wicker Park, experience racial conflict. And residents in both neighborhoods perceive a nonresponsive city bureaucracy. Complaints about inadequate city services, police harassment, and discrimination in the schools are pervasive. However, although the problem descriptions are similar, the levels of concern exhibited in Philadelphia neighborhoods are considerably below those of the two Chicago neighborhoods. This may be because the problems in the former are in fact less severe, either because they are compounded by lower levels of crime, or because Philadelphia residents have available superior problem-solving resources.

Sunset stands out as an area with minimal concerns about the surveyed indicators of social disorganization. However, two situations perceived as a threat to neighborhood integrity were identified in the field data. The first is a change in the commercial area. One local businessman explained that the problem is posed not so much by the new businesses coming in, but rather by the loss of small neighborhood enterprises. "We lose our identity when we lose our small merchants."

The second and more pressing concern is the perception of the area's deprived position as a recipient of city services. Although it is a relatively affluent area, residents complain about inadequate police protection, inadequate bus service, inadequate recreation facilities, and inadequate allocation of community development funds. Most respondents felt that they were not getting a fair return for their tax dollars.

According to Sunset activists, although voting turnout is high, relations with the Board of Supervisors, San Francisco's elected legislature, is poor. "We can't get to them," noted one neighborhood activist.

> The Sunset is a forgotten community. We don't get an equitable proportion of resources. We elect the supervisors, decide every ballot, then they forget us.

Conclusions

The residents in these ten neighborhoods vary not only in the signs of incivility they confront, but also in the ways that they respond to essentially comparable conditions. To some extent this can be accounted for by the changes occurring in the area at any given time. Although all neighborhoods experience some degree of change most of the time, they vary in the extent to which some changes occur, in the direction they take, and in the time frame within which they take place. New groups of people move in, while others leave. Old housing stock deteriorates. New housing is constructed. Commercial areas decline or change in character. New ones may be introduced. In some instances, some areas disappear entirely. Recreation facilities, social services, and other amenities may expand, decline, or be removed entirely.

In some of our neighborhoods, these changes have been minor, often barely noticeable. In others they have extended over longer periods of time so that the immediate impact is not so readily apparent. And in some they have been rapid and clearly visible. For the most part, these transformations reflect the larger movements of population and business that have affected major urban centers through the years. Most frequently this has involved the exodus of the more affluent White population and the entry of low income minorities. Recently, however, in some neighborhoods this process has been reversed as more affluent professionals move into areas populated mainly by low-income minorities. Our examination of the concerns of neighborhood residents suggests that such changes shape the responses to and interpretations of local conditions. We look next at the statistically documented population movements and at the residents' perception of change in the ten research sites.

Neighborhood Change

In devising measures for population stability, we defined as stable those areas with a substantial portion of long-time residents and a relatively small percentage of recent arrivals. In Figure 5 we see the percentage of the residents in each category in the ten neighborhoods. By these measures South Philadelphia stands out as the area that has sustained the smallest amount of population movement. The short-term residents measure indicates that six out of ten neighborhoods have experienced substantial population change. In three of these neighborhoods, Mission, Lincoln Park, and Logan, over half of the residents have lived in the area for five years or less.

Figure 6 documents perceptions of change in the neighborhoods. Although the rankings in the two figures are not identical, the fact that the same neighborhoods lie on the high and low ends of these measures suggests that, for most people, neighborhoods change means population movement. Two anomalies should be noted here: The position of Back of the Yards on the stability perception measure is a good deal higher than its position on the long- and short-term residents measure would suggest. And Sunset's image as a stable neighborhood reflected in its position on the long-term residents and perception measure is belied by the large percentage of short-term residents in the area. The long-term residents in this case are the sizable numbers of older people who have raised their families and plan to remain in the area. The more recent arrivals are predominantly younger Oriental families, who have purchased homes in the neighborhood.

An examination of the views on the direction of change indicates that most of the residents are pessimistic about the future of the neighborhoods. Wicker Park and Logan are notable in the large percentage of

FIGURE 5
Population Stability

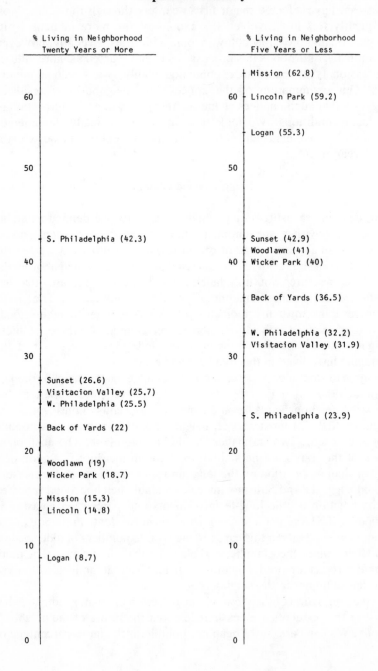

FIGURE 6
Perception of Neighborhood Change

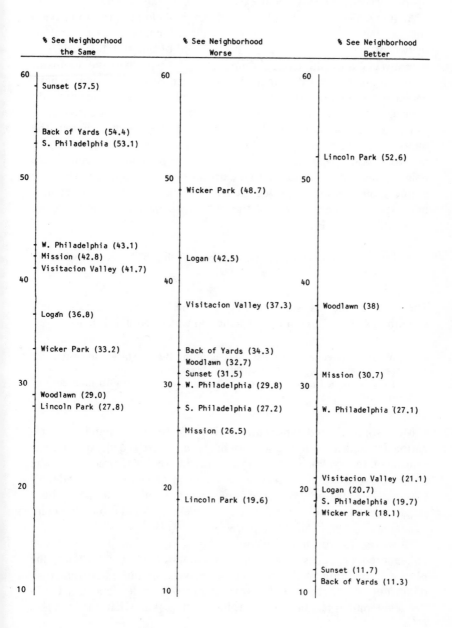

residents perceiving neighborhood decline. In Woodlawn equal portions of the residents saw their neighborhood moving in opposite directions. Only in Lincoln Park and Mission does the percentage of residents noting improvement exceed those noting decline.

Again we need to look at the data from the field research to provide some insight into the context in which these opinions were generated. In two of the neighborhoods at the low end of our stability measure, recent racial and ethnic population movement is seen as the dominant factor in neighborhood change. Both Wicker Park and Logan experienced substantial racial transition in the 1960s and 1970s, significantly altering both the ethnic and age distribution of neighborhood residents. In both areas the remaining Whites tended to be elderly, whereas the minorities coming in were younger families with children. In both neighborhoods residents also associated the population change with neighborhood deterioration. Two explanations were offered. The new ethnic groups were perceived as not sharing the same maintenance interests and commitments of the older residents. An elderly Polish woman in Wicker Park noted:

> This neighborhood used to be nice, but now it is bad. The sidewalks are terrible and there is garbage all over.

The cause for all this, she claimed, was "the Puerto Ricans who don't keep things clean." A similar explanation was offered in Logan:

> We didn't have any problems here until the Blacks started to come. . . .
> There wasn't any graffiti or roaches, or rats. . . .
> They brought them with them. They don't know how to take care of anything.

More sophisticated explanations were offered by community organization activists in both neighborhoods, who blamed the physical deterioration on the decline in city services and the redlining practices of the financial institutions that frequently occur in neighborhoods undergoing racial transition. Whatever the cause, residents in both these neighborhoods noted extensive racial and ethnic population movement accompanied by physical deterioration.

However, for residents in Wicker Park, physical improvement also engendered concerns. Housing rehabilitation, while improving the physical condition of the neighborhood, was pricing its current residents out of the area. Thus, many organization leaders noted that "redevelopment has become a problem worse than what it is trying to solve." Indeed, in Wicker Park many organization leaders saw the deterioration of the neighborhood as part of a covert plan by the city administration to drive out the current residents and make way for a higher-income group that could afford to support the newly rehabilitated housing.

Wicker Park residents are afraid that their neighborhood will become another Lincoln Park. There the changes, we have seen, led to neighborhood improvement. But it was improvement undertaken at the expense of the low-income minority residents who were driven out of the area by urban renewal programs in the 1960s. The current inhabitants have benefited from the physical improvement of the neighborhood and the population transformation that drove minority low-income residents out and brought in the more well-to-do, White professionals who currently reside there.

Woodlawn has experienced no racial transition in recent years. But it has suffered a 30 percent population decrease in the past ten years, which residents say was caused primarily by serious gang violence and extensive arson fires. These are also associated with the departure of most of the commercial enterprises providing an economic base for the area. Because these problems were most severe in the early 1970s, many residents now see their neighborhood getting better. Those who claim the area is getting worse note the population decline, the physical deterioration caused by arson and housing abandonments, and the commercial deterioration.

Changes in Mission, as indicated by Figures 4 and 5, were differentially perceived. The population movement there appears to be part of the same *gentrification* process that has occurred in Lincoln Park and is feared in Wicker Park. Housing renovation and area redevelopment is seen by the White residents as an indication of neighborhood improvement and stability; whereas the minorities, who cannot afford the rents and rising property values, see it as an effort to remove them and change the character of the neighborhood. "It's like they don't want us around." The changes in the commercial areas of Mission are viewed as threatening by the older merchants and adjacent residents.

In Sunset the ethnic diversity introduced by the Orientals is even more prevalent in the commercial areas. For the most part, small owner-operated businesses with long histories in the area have dominated these strips. In the past these merchants were American born. More recently, however, they have been joined by Armenians, Indians, and Chinese. Furthermore, there were also some changes in the types of businesses coming in and they for the most part have been unwelcome. One area businessman noted, "the merchants make a community. If they are good, then so is the community." What is considered good are the small stores whose owners are committed to the neighborhood. Some of these have been replaced recently by large savings and loan companies and chain stores, such as Kentucky Fried Chicken. These are considered undesirable because they constitute a threat to the character of the neighborhood.

The other four neighborhoods in this study experienced less extensive changes. In many instances, as in the racial transition that transformed both Woodlawn and West Philadelphia, the changes occurred less recently and apparently less rapidly. Back of the Yards' image as a stable community may derive less from the population movement, which has been fairly extensive, than from the fact the 70 percent of the respondents in the survey reported that they expected to remain in the area. In addition, although the population has changed, the majority of the newer residents share the values and perceptions of the old-timers. "We're still basically an immigrant community with good kids and strict and caring parents."

In South Philadelphia as well little has changed. There, even the young people who generally move out of city neighborhoods tend to remain. One respondent noted that only two people out of his high school class have left the area. This perception of stability in these two neighborhoods provides a measure of comfort to area residents and makes it possible for them to tolerate conditions that in other settings might be seen as symptoms of neighborhood decay.

In examining the impact of neighborhood context on the levels of fear and concern reported by area residents, we need to look not only at those contextual variables that we have defined as indicators of incivility, but also at the population composition and levels of change characterizing the neighborhoods in which they are found. These, as much as the conditions themselves, play a role in shaping the responses and interpretations of neighborhood residents. Loitering teenagers and even physical decay tend to produce more anxiety when they are associated with the intrusion of strangers into a neighborhood. And this anxiety is compounded when the intrusion is rapid and extensive and when the long-term residents are elderly and the newcomers are young.

Crime, Incivility, and Fear

In Figure 7 we compare measures of aggregated concern and incivility indicators with the percentage of residents reporting fear in the neighborhoods. We note first that in eight of the neighborhoods,

FIGURE 7
Crime, Incivility and Fear

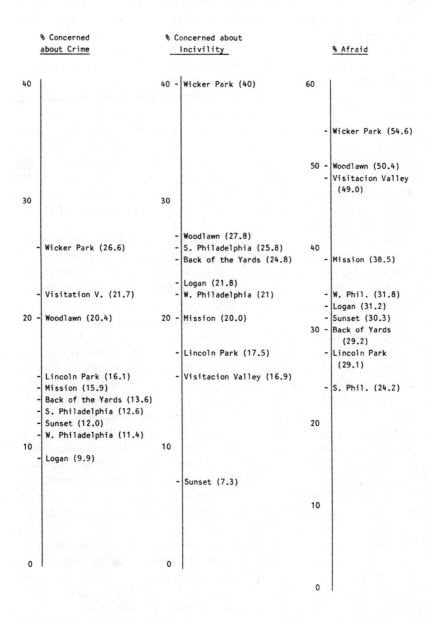

% Concerned
about Crime

% Concerned about
Incivility

% Afraid

40

40 - Wicker Park (40)

60

- Wicker Park (54.6)

50 - Woodlawn (50.4)
- Visitacion Valley
  (49.0)

30

30

- Woodlawn (27.8)
- S. Philadelphia (25.8)
- Back of the Yards (24.8)

40

- Mission (38.5)

- Wicker Park (26.6)

- Logan (21.8)
- W. Philadelphia (21)

- Visitation V. (21.7)

- W. Phil. (31.8)
- Logan (31.2)

20 - Woodlawn (20.4)

20 - Mission (20.0)

- Sunset (30.3)

30 - Back of Yards
  (29.2)

- Lincoln Park (17.5)

- Lincoln Park
  (29.1)

- Lincoln Park (16.1)
- Mission (15.9)
- Back of the Yards (13.6)
- S. Philadelphia (12.6)
- Sunset (12.0)
- W. Philadelphia (11.4)

- Visitacion Valley (16.9)

- S. Phil. (24.2)

20

10

- Logan (9.9)

10

- Sunset (7.3)

10

0

0

0

residents' concerns about incivility exceed their concerns about crime. Visitacion Valley and Sunset are the only exceptions in this regard. Second, we see that in each neighborhood the percentage of residents reporting fear exceed both those exhibiting concerns about crime and concerns about incivility.

In all these neighborhoods, a relatively small percentage of the residents actually have vicitimization experiences. Others are indirectly affected by their knowledge of those experiences, acquired either through informal communications networks or through the media. In addition, as we have seen, there are a number of other situations, including population change, the incivility concerns tapped in the telephone survey and those identified in the field data, that area residents interpret as threats to their well-being. The latter include racial conflict, deterioration in commercial areas or changes in the character of the business establishments, neighborhood improvements threatening to drive out low-income residents, and perceived inadequacies in city services.

The fact that fear levels exceed those measuring both crime awareness and crime concern might be due in most neighborhoods to the compounding effect of the other incivility concerns. Thus, perceptions of increases in crime are continually reinforced by other visible reminders that the community is changing in threatening ways.

This explanation is not as convincing in Lincoln Park, Visitacion Valley, and Sunset, where incivility indicators are less visible and extensive. Although residents in Visitacion Valley and, to a lesser extent, those in Lincoln Park confront more pervasive crime, they do not face the constant visible reminders of neighborhood decay found in many of the other areas. Residents in Sunset, on the other hand, report neither serious crime nor social disorganization concerns. One must ask them, why do fear levels in Visitacion Valley approximate those in Woodlawn and Wicker Park, where high crime combines with pervasive indicators of physical and social deterioration to create the most seriously troubled neighborhoods? And why, given the demographic similarities between the two neighborhoods, are fear levels in Sunset equal to those in Lincoln Park where crime is so much more pervasive?

Indeed, the cluster of neighborhoods around the 30 percent mark on the fear measure raise some intriguing questions. These areas differ on a number of demographic dimensions generally associated with variations in fear. White, affluent neighborhoods like Lincoln Park and Sunset are generally expected to generate lower fear levels than low-income Black or transitional areas like West Philadelphia and Logan. The more pervasive crime in Lincoln Park might explain its position in that cluster. And, given the positive relation of age and fear, the elderly population in Sunset might explain the similarity in fear levels of Sunset and Lincoln Park. But this cannot explain Sunset's similarity with West Philadelphia, where there is an equally large elderly population that is both Black and low-income and faces more serious problems. Given what we know about the relationship of fear, vicitimization experiences, and demographic characteristics, we would expect to find more fear in Lincoln Park, Logan, and West Philadelphia than in Sunset.

It is difficult to explain Sunset's position in this cluster by just asking what makes people afraid, because the conditions perceived as fear-inducing appear to be sparse indeed. If we turn the question around, however, and ask what makes people feel secure, other considerations come to the fore. This turns our attention to resources that enhance the capabilities of neighborhood residents to cope with the problems they confront. These resources, we argue, make it possible to exercise social control and thus foster a sense of security, among neighborhood residents, mediating threatening changes and the anxiety that such changes induce. Since most urban communities experience social change as a constant, the issue of fear is affected by the community's capacity to regulate and deal with that change. Neighborhood residents with adequate resources are able to cope with extensive transformations, whereas those without them might find even minimal changes frightening. We apply this premise next in our examination of the sources of social control in each of the ten sites.

6

Sources of Social Control

Communities with a high degree of social control have some assurance that (1) residents adhere to a shared set of expectations about appropriate behavior; (2) private property is kept up in accordance with commonly accepted standards; (3) public areas are adequately maintained; and (4) access is regulated so as to control the incursion of population groups, private enterprises, and public institutions that are perceived to threaten the integrity of the neighborhood.

The first two items reflect the moral order of the community. In neighborhoods where the majority of the residents share common backgrounds, where there is minimal population movement, and where there is a high level of informal social interaction, commonly held norms are more likely to be held and enforced. The last two items reflect the political order of the community. To secure city services and to control access to the community, local residents must have the capacity to influence municipal service bureaucracies and both the public and private decision-making agencies that play a role in determining the direction of neighborhood change.

The effective exercise of social control, thus, depends to some extent on the individual attributes of neighborhood residents and, to some extent, on their interactions in both formal and informal settings. On the one hand, an individual attribute such as home ownership provides opportunities for controlling neighborhood property that are not available to renters. High levels of income and/or education tend to enhance the capacity of local residents to pursue neighborhood interests through political means. On the other hand, extensive, informal, social interaction facilitates the transmission of common values and engenders a sense of belonging and community attachment that strengthens the moral order of the community. In neighborhoods where such interaction does not naturally emerge, it can be fostered artificially by formally organized community groups (Hunter 1975). Although such groups are generally formed for specific problem-solving purposes more relevant to strengthening the political resources of the community, they also frequently stimulate the informal interactions that strengthen the moral order. We will consider both the formally organized groups and the informal social interactions of neighborhood residents to be measures of social integration and sources of social control in the community.

In assessing the social control resources of the ten neighborhoods, we will consider: (1) the demographic characteristics of local residents, (2) the perceived ability of local activists to generate response from bureaucratic and political agencies, (3) neighborhood support systems provided by high levels of informal integration, (4) and the perceived effectiveness of local groups in involving neighborhood residents and in solving local problems.

Our assessment of the organizational and political strength of each community is based on the unstructured interviews conducted by our field workers with a wide range of activists in each of the neighborhoods. The fifteen months in the field made it possible for us to characterize the political and organizational resources of the neighborhoods with a reasonable degree of accuracy. Our assessment of social integration is based on two measures derived from the survey data. The first is a measure of formal integration reflected in the percentage of respondents reporting involvement in community affairs. The second is a measure of the informal interaction of community residents with each other.

In developing the informal integration measure, we considered the following six items in our survey:

1. In general is it pretty easy or pretty difficult for you to tell a stranger in your neighborhood from somebody who lives here?
2. Would you say that you really feel a part of your neighborhood or do you think of it more as just a place to live?
3. How about kids in your immediate neighborhood? How many of them do you know by name: all of them, some, hardly any, or none of them?
4. How many years have you personally lived in the neighborhood?
5. Do you own your home or do you rent it?
6. Do you expect to be living in this neighborhood two years from now?

Items such as these have been assumed to reflect a unidimensional construct of social integration. However, a factor analysis by Riger and Lavrakas (1981) revealed two distinct dimensions. Items *1, 2,* and *3* represent the extent to which respondents have formed social bonds within their community. Items *4, 5,* and *6* represent residential rootedness. The correlation between the two items was .58, indicating that those who have lived in a community for a longer period of time are also more likely to form social bonds.

In computing these two variables for each respondent, Riger and Lavrakas found that while 66 percent of the respondents were either high or low on both dimensions, 34 percent fell into the off-diagonal categories. Of particular interest to our analysis are those who score high on residential rootedness, but low on social bonds. These frequently tend to be elderly residents who live in a changing neighborhood and do not have the resources to leave (Riger and Lavrakas 1981; Skogan and Maxfield 1980). And because these are exactly the respondents who tend to be most fearful and benefit least from the support system that residential stability might provide under other circumstances, we have deleted the measure for residential rootedness in our assessment of informal social integration and utilized only those items measuring social bonds. We have also ignored measures that indicate extra-community network relationships (Wellman 1977), because such relationships cannot provide the territorially specific support that might alleviate fear of crime.

The three social bondedness items measuring informal social integration for our analysis were combined to form an additive index with an alpha coefficient of .585. In order to make this scale more amenable to the purposes of descriptive analyses to be reported here, the social integration scale was collapsed to three categories using cut points that resulted in an approximately normal distribution of values (i.e., about 50 percent of the cases falling into the middle category and about 25 percent each into the low or the high categories). Thus, the scale was recoded to indicate levels of integration that could be termed quantitatively as *low, moderate,* and *high*.

Table 5 presents the resulting distribution of respondents categorized according to low, moderate, and high levels of social integration. Figure 8 shows the fear levels in each neighborhood as a function of the level of social integration. With the exception of Sunset, social integration is associated with lower fear levels in all neighborhoods and appears to serve as a support system granting a measure of security to community residents.

Although we examined all of the sources of social control separately, we realize that frequently the possession of some facilitates the acquisition of others. For example, higher status individuals are more efficacious and exhibit greater ability to control the environment in which they live (Verba and Nie 1974). However, these characteristics also induce higher levels of organizational participation. On the other hand, we have evidence that there are situations that can induce low-

TABLE 5
Percent Distribution of Respondents
According to Degree of Social Integration

Level of Social Integration	Chicago				
	Lincoln Park	Wicker Park	Woodlawn	Back of the Yards	City
Low	21.9	14.8	19.6	8.5	18.5
Moderate	60.1	61.0	54.1	57.8	51.5
High	18.1	24.1	26.2	33.8	30.0
	(310)	(260)	(106)	(124)	(379)

	Philadelphia			
	West Philadelphia	South Philadelphia	Logan	City
Low	10.1	4.9	11.2	11.9
Moderate	49.1	43.1	51.3	48.8
High	40.7	51.9	37.5	39.2
	(224)	(253)	(165)	(424)

	San Francisco			
	Sunset	Visitacion Valley	Mission	City
Low	20.6	17.9	32.1	27.8
Moderate	58.4	58.0	52.5	54.9
High	21.1	24.1	15.4	17.4
	(275)	(252)	(182)	(439)

*The number in the parentheses gives the total N for that neighborhood.

FIGURE 8

Fear by Level of Social Integration

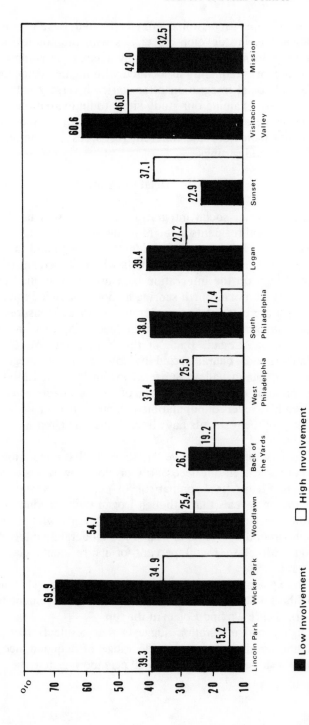

status groups to organize effectively and this, in some instances, enables them to develop closer ties with the political establishment. Although formal integration via involvement in community organizations is more frequently associated with higher socioeconomic status, informal social integration often varies inversely with it. We expect then, as we examine our study sites, to find variations not only in the extensiveness of the resources available, but also in the ways in which incivility indicators and different resources are combined in specific neighborhood settings.

Social Integration

Our informal social integration construct was used to categorize neighborhood residents as high, moderate, or low integrates. Figure 9 presents the distribution of residents with high and low scores in the ten neighborhoods. Neighborhoods where 50 percent of the residents scored high on the integration measure are classified as high; those with less than one-fourth scoring high are classified low, and those in-between are classified as moderate. By these measures we have one highly integrated area—South Philadelphia; four moderates—West Philadelphia, Logan, Back of the Yards, and Woodlawn; and five neighborhoods characterized by low levels of integration—Wicker Park, Visitacion Valley, Sunset, Lincoln Park, and Mission. With the exception of Visitacion Valley, all of the *low integration* neighborhoods exhibit high levels of population instability. In each instance 40 percent or more of the residents have lived in their neighborhoods five years or less.

The case of Logan, however, suggests that population instability in and of itself need not necessarily produce low levels of social integration. In Figure 10 a comparison of population instability and social integration reveals that although Logan ranks second only to Mission in the percentage (55.3 percent) of residents who have lived in the neighborhood five years or less, it is a moderately integrated neighborhood with close to 40 percent of its residents classified as high integrates.

An explanation for this can be found in Figure 11, which ranks the neighborhoods by percentage of resident involvement in community affairs. There we find Logan at the top.

High social integration suggests that residents feel a part of the neighborhood and have a wide range of acquaintances there. This could well result from informal neighboring activities that tend to

FIGURE 9
Levels of Social Integration

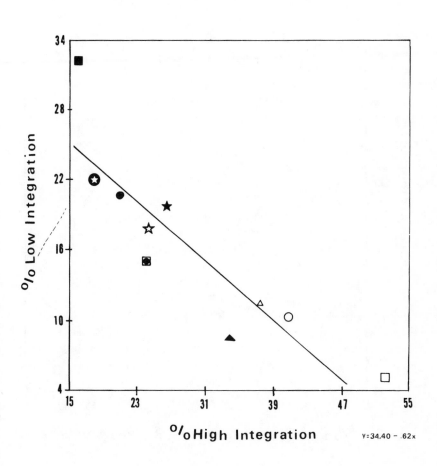

Legend

○ West Philadelphia   ▲ Back of the Yards
□ South Philadelphia   ★ Woodlawn
△ Logan   ☆ Visitacion Valley
✪ Lincoln Park   ● Sunset
▣ Wicker Park   ■ Mission

FIGURE 10
Population Stability and Integration

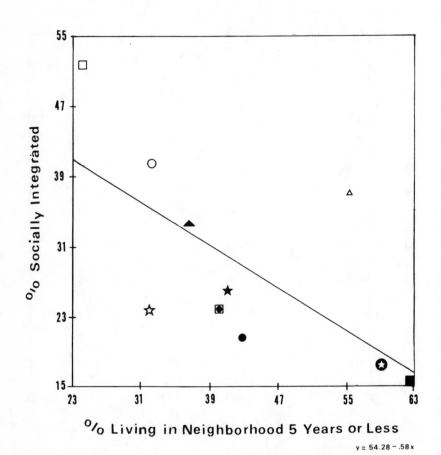

% Socially Integrated

% Living in Neighborhood 5 Years or Less

y = 54.28 - .58x

Legend

○ West Philadelphia   ▲ Back of the Yards
□ South Philadelphia   ★ Woodlawn
△ Logan   ☆ Visitacion Valley
✪ Lincoln Park   ● Sunset
▣ Wicker Park   ■ Mission

FIGURE 11
Percent Involved in Community Affairs

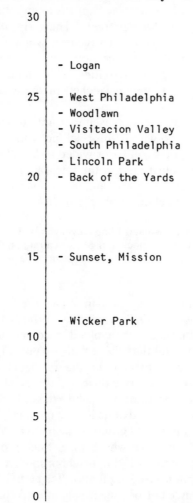

```
30

                - Logan

25              - West Philadelphia
                - Woodlawn
                - Visitacion Valley
                - South Philadelphia
                - Lincoln Park
20              - Back of the Yards



15              - Sunset, Mission


                - Wicker Park
10



 5



 0
```

increase with long-term residence in an area. But it can also be induced by participation in formally organized community organizations.

In either case such integration seems to provide a support system for neighborhood residents who feel more comfortable in a community where they know people to whom they can turn for help when needed. South Philadelphia provides ample illustration of the informal support provided in a stable neighborhood where long-term residency is the norm and cooperative neighboring the expected mode of behavior. "Here in South Philadelphia we take care of our own . . . . We are like a family, not neighbors. If something happens to me, the people who did it would have to fight the whole street." These strong community ties also induce an unusual level of attentiveness, which was illustrated for our field worker when she was questioned by two neighborhood men who had been observing her activities. This incident confirmed her feeling "that everyone is being watched in these narrow streets in South Philadelphia."

Formal organizations are not as important to socially integrated residents. But in areas where informal networks do not develop naturally, similar supports can be provided by small-scale community organizations. This is illustrated in the integration that appears to be fostered by such groups in Logan and in the following statement of a West Philadelphia block club member:

> On my block I'm known and I know everybody. I can feel safe walking on my block at twelve o'clock at night. I'm afraid on the bus, but when I reach my neighborhood I'm not afraid because the people I know around here, know me.

This sense of belonging may explain in part the findings reported in Schneider and Schneider (1977), Lavrakas (1978), and Kidder, Cohn, and Harvey (1978) that citizens involved in community organizations are less likely to be fearful than those who are not. Figure 11 indicates that between 20 and 27 percent of the residents in seven of the neighborhoods are likely to derive the benefits associated with community involvement. In Sunset, Mission, and Wicker Park, however, such involvement and the related advantages are minimal.

Association with community groups appears to have some impact on the sense of security of those who belong. Such groups, if effective, also serve as a resource for the neighborhood at large. When a community organization has a reputation for getting things done and when concrete examples of organizational effectiveness are visible in the neighborhood, the group may well impart to all the residents the feeling there is in fact some mechanism available for controlling what happens in the area. In such areas, even nonmembers with problems tend to turn to the community organization for help.

Organizational Strength

Table 6 indicates the variations in the perceptions of organizational strength. These classifications reflect our interpretations of the assess-

TABLE 6
Perceived Organizational Effectiveness

High	Moderate	Low
Back of the Yards	West Philadelphia	Sunset
Lincoln Park	South Philadelphia	Mission
Logan		Wicker Park
Woodlawn		
Visitacion Valley		

ments made by a wide range of local activists in the area. The organizations classified as high are perceived as viable by activists either because they attract an active working membership or because they have adequate funds and staff to support their activities. They also serve as effective umbrella groups coordinating the activities of a number of disparate organizations in the area. Such groups were found in Back of the Yards, Lincoln Park, Logan, Woodlawn, and Visitacion Valley. Organizations classified as moderate attract an active membership and have at least adequate financial resources; however, they are not able to effectively coordinate the activities of other groups in the area. Such groups exist in West and South Philadelphia.

Within the West Philadelphia borders are five local civic associations, a multitude of block clubs and three umbrella groups all attempting unsuccessfully to unite in an effort to more effectively achieve their common goals. However, the competition among these groups for scarce city funds and the apparent jealousy among the leaders have prevented the formation of a working coalition. In South Philadelphia there are a large number of groups activated only sporadically as crises emerged in the community. Efforts to coordinate activities have also failed here, in part because the informal support system provided by the high level of social integration in the neighborhood makes a more formalized network less necessary.

Activists in Sunset, Mission, and Wicker Park implicitly ranked the effectiveness of their organizations as poor. Sunset residents defy the accepted political science wisdom that associates high socioeconomic status with high levels of participation. Unlike the residents in the other high-income neighborhood in this study, they have not translated their educational and economic advantage into organizational effectiveness. Although there are in Sunset a number of organizations attempting to address community problems, levels of involvement are low and funding and staff support is minimal. Sunset activists consider this to be a major problem and a cause of their neighborhood's neglect by the city's political and bureaucratic establishment.

> Everything is isolated in the Sunset. There's no Sunset community. The result is no pressure group.

In Mission, involvement is also low in the large number of groups addressing the problems identified by residents. These groups are fragmented and often work at cross purposes. This is due in part to the diverse interests of the heterogeneous population. Thus, one group's solution is likely to become another group's problem. The young, White professionals are more likely to push for neighborhood redevelopment, which creates serious difficulties for the minorities who cannot afford the subsequent rental and real estate increases. Minorities on the other hand are more concerned with the deep-seated economic and cultural adjustment problems. Whites are more likely to be associated with neighborhood improvement and block clubs that address issues that are more readily resolved, whereas minorities depend more on the work of the social service agencies that provide temporary relief from distress caused by external forces they are powerless to control.

In assessing organizational effectiveness, middle-class professionals in Mission saw some reason for optimism. Their success in redevelopment and housing rehabilitation efforts suggested that intensive organizational activities achieved results. This was particularly true because forces external to the area were working for goals consistent with their needs and interests. The minorities in Mission fared less well. Their organizational contact was primarily with service agencies that centered on a client-professional rather than a self-help relationship. Their problems also were less amendable to quick solutions and were, in fact, aggravated by the redevelopment projects designed to deal with the difficulties confronting the middle-class residents of Mission.

Wicker Park ranks at the bottom of all the sites in the percentage of residents involved in community organizations (see Figure 11). As in Mission, the neighborhood groups are dominated by Whites. Although several of them address issues of interest to the minority residents, and although they tend to support the minorities in their concern about redevelopment and gentrification, they have not been successful in recruiting a significant number of members from the Latino community. The Alinsky umbrella group in the area has hired White organizers who claim little success in energizing local residents. "People have to be encouraged to take action. They won't work for themselves."

The effectively organized neighborhoods represent a range of socioeconomic and ethnic profiles that are reflected in the circumstances prompting the formation of their dominant umbrella organizations and in the issues currently addressed. Racial and ethnically heterogeneous, predominantly White, predominantly Black neighborhoods, and the major income groups are represented in this grouping.

Four out of the five groups in these areas were created with the help of a community organizer. The Back of the Yards Council and The Woodlawn Organization (TWO) were organized under the tutelage of Saul Alinsky. The Back of the Yards Council is the oldest and most powerful group identified in this study. Created in 1938 to help solve the social and economic problems of the packinghouse workers who live in the area, the council today is committed to maintaining the physical environment of the neighborhood and serving its predominantly White working-class clientele. Supported by substantial funding, a long-term, committed membership, and the prestige and political connections of its executive director, it coordinates the activities of all of the institutions in the neighborhood.

The Woodlawn Organization (TWO), founded in 1960 to oppose the expansion of the University of Chicago's South Campus, dominates the organizational life of its neighborhood. Most of the organizations and block clubs in the area are affiliated with TWO, which currently is committed to "restructuring Woodlawn physically, economically, and socially." Like the Back of the Yards Council, TWO has become a neighborhood institution. Supported by a staff of about 200 and financed by a number of major foundations, it offers a variety of social support services for welfare recipients, senior citizens, and the unemployed. Its major focus currently is on economic development in the area. And although both staff and community residents claim that this emphasis is taking attention away from the severe social problems still plaguing the community, the results are clearly visible to all who view its housing developments, supermarket, and movie theater. Some residents feel that the organization has moved away from its grassroots base. But its position in the community and its achievements provide clear evidence that local residents can exert some control in dealing with local problems.

The All People's Coalition in Visitacion Valley is a more recently organized group that still utilizes the Alinsky type confrontation tactics no longer needed by the two older organizations. Although it does not have the strength of the older groups, it is credited with bringing a major crime prevention program into the community and has generally built a reputation as the place to go when things need to get done. The director of a neighborhood service center described the APC's position as a linkage mechanism. "If we have mice on the playgound or leaks in the plumbing, we call them (APC) and they get on the city's case to get over and fix it. It's pretty good."

Logan's rich organizational life is reflected in its position as first among all sites in the percentage of residents involved in community affairs (27 percent). Organizational life there is dominated by the racially integrated Ad Hoc Committee for Logan, which was formed specifically to deal with the myriad of problems created by the racial and economic changes in the area. Under its umbrella are found approximately sixty block clubs and a number of area religious and service organizations. Its three major committees—housing, youth, and safety—address in some way all the major problems in the neighborhoods. Concrete evidence of this group's success is seen in the improved lighting and tree pruning services in the area.

The heart of the committee's activity, however, consists in block club organizing. As one leader put it, "it became apparent to us in a large community like Logan that unless a small unit by unit method of organization was used, any attempt at organizing would be futile." The block clubs enable the Ad Hoc Committee to address both the physical and social deterioration of the area. They form the mechanism by which membership is recruited and, thus, provide the power base needed for the pressure tactics applied to the city bureaucracy and other relevant institutions. They also work to bring together a seriously divided community. Organization members claim that racial integration has proceeded more smoothly in Logan than in other Philadelphia communities precisely because the block clubs have managed to open up communications between previously hostile groups. The social integration that was so severely disrupted by the rapid population and economic changes in this formerly homogeneous neighborhood appears to be reemerging, at least among the members of the Ad Hoc Committee, as a function of their joint efforts in community problem-solving. "Through fighting and victories, a sense of pride has been developed and there is a real sense of togetherness among the people."

Unlike the groups in the other four sites, the Lincoln Park Conservation Association (LPCA), an umbrella organization coordinating the activities of several smaller neighborhood groups in the area, is committed to maintaining the benefits that have already been derived. Formed in the 1950s when the city's urban renewal program began the process that was to transform the community from a deteriorating neighborhood to one of the most exclusive areas in the city, the LPCA was intent on participating in the urban renewal decisions. Its members were the beneficiaries of these decisions and for the most part lacked the concern about minority displacement evident in Wicker Park and Mission. LPCA concentrates on neighborhood beautification, crime prevention, and other activities designed to "defend" its area from external influences that might create additional problems for the residents. Thus, efforts were made to keep out of the area a game room that they felt would attract "outside" teenagers and a supermarket that might bring in a clientele from a nearby low-income housing project.

The residents in the communities served by these five groups differ in the kinds and the severity of problems they confront and in the quality and number of other resources available to them. But they all share access to a community institution that has produced visible signs of effectiveness and that is viewed by members and nonmembers alike as the place to go when help is needed. As such, these groups serve not only as local problem-solving agencies, but also as symbolic evidence that some degree of local control is possible.

Relations With City Bureaucrats

Many of the tasks undertaken by these groups require the cooperation of city service agency bureaucrats. The variations in the character of the relationship with these officials described by the activists in these neighborhoods suggests that effective organizations do not necessarily produce cooperative relations with city bureaucrats, local police, and elected officials. Leaders in only three of the neighborhoods reported positive relations. In four others, they described an adversary relationship that could produce response when appropriate tactics were employed. And in three communities, the politically alienated leadership perceived hostile, unresponsive officials who could not be influenced.

The political support provided by the residents of South Philadelphia and Back of the Yards to the dominant party organizations in Philadelphia and Chicago respectively ensured, in their view, positive responses from the service bureaucracies to their demands. Residents in both neighborhoods were statisfied both with the level of police protection and with the allocation of other city services in their neighborhoods. An early battle with Chicago's Democratic organizations ended with a victory for the Back of the Yards Council, which produced a cooperative relationship between the two that endures to this day. Council program implementation has been facilitated by easy access to information about the ownership of homes and real estate in the area, the cooperation of the fire department in an effort to reduce electrical fires in the area, and the cooperation of the local police who refer young people picked up on misdemeanor charges to the Back of the Yards Council's youth guidance project. The effectiveness of the Council's control over the environment was illustrated in a recent study of Chicago code violations, which found not only that this area ranked first in the number of violations reported, but also that this constituted twice as many as were reported by the area ranked second (Jones 1979).

Although residents in Lincoln Park do not support the dominant political organization, their political sophistication and that of the independent alderman whom they elect, as well as the status and effectiveness of their neighborhood groups, has engendered a working relationship with city agencies that assures adequate support for the neighborhood.

Residents in Logan, Visitacion Valley, West Philadelphia, and Woodlawn, who claim no ties to the political establishment, define city service agencies as adversaries who must be forced to do their jobs. These relationships, as well as the tactics required to produce a response to neighborhood demands, were clearly spelled out by Logan residents. Unable to rely on the traditional ties with the locally elected officials who serve as intermediaries between their constituents and the service bureaucracy that serves them, they developed an alternative neighborhood power base. This power base engenders a relationship with the political establishment that is both qualitatively and quantitatively different from that prevailing in areas that are well connected politically. Neighborhood organizations have to fight for the services that one phone call from a powerful committeeman in Philadelphia or the director of the Back of the Yards Council can provide. In describing the battle to get the trees in Logan pruned, one respondent stated:

> Though there was a constant harranguement, petitioning of the people at the park office, we had to circumvent the political hierarchy to finally get this done. Now very few streets have not been tackled. But its an ongoing war that we have and will continue to wage.

Thus, the political process, rather than being a smooth transmission of requests to elected officials eliciting response, is seen as an ongoing battle. Those who are elected or appointed to serve are seen as the adversaries rather than the servants of the people.

This feeling was shared in the other neighborhoods. In West Philadelphia the city was described as uncaring and disinterested in the
community. "The city doesn't care too much about the inner-city
people." A city council member urged the local organization to unite so
they could *extract* concessions from the city. In Visitacion Valley,
where the APC organized a mass confrontation with the Board of
Supervisors to elicit its neighborhood's participation in a pilot crime
prevention program, one respondent echoed the views expressed in
Logan. "The only power you have is the power of the people. And
"we've got to push, push, push, to get things done." And in Woodlawn
the same tactics were invoked. Although TWO does not have the
power of the Back of the Yards Council, it can produce a crowd to
bring pressure on the Board of Education to protest court delays and to
push for the prosecution of neighborhood drug dealers.

Although activists in these neighborhoods felt that they were engaged in an ongoing battle with city bureaucracies, they did claim some
victories. And these engendered a sense of confidence that, difficult as
the task may be, there are tactics that can elicit bureaucratic response
and will enable local residents to influence the developments in their
neighborhoods.

This feeling was not shared by activists in Sunset and Wicker Park
and by the leaders of minority organizations in Mission. Lacking both
political power and organizational strength, they spoke of their inability to elicit the kind of services that might make a visible impact in their
neighborhoods. In Mission and Wicker Park, residents who feared
being displaced by the redevelopment planned for their areas noted
that the only improvements in their neighborhoods were made at the
expense of those who currently live there and for the benefit of those
who will ultimately move in. As one Mission resident put it: "People
who are planning to revamp the shopping area are flippant and cavalier
about the people who live there." In Wicker Park activists accuse city
officials and local realtors of complicity in the arson epidemic, which is
viewed as part of a larger effort to clear the area for eventual *gentrification*.

Residents in all three neighborhoods complain about inadequate
police services. In Wicker Park and in Mission, police harrassment of
residents is an equally serious concern. One Wicker Park resident
expressed a feeling common in both areas: "Police will hassle you, but
will not deal with our problems." In all three communities, activists
note that they are ignored and manipulated. In Mission, a local
merchant explaining the deterioration of the local business district
stated, "City Hall does not want to do anything and that's all that
matters." And in Sunset there is a feeling that the neighborhood is

victimized by its low crime rate. "We have less crime, but also less of everything else, less police, less government participation."

All of these problems are aggravated by the sense that this insensitivity is deliberate. A young White project resident in Mission argued that the problems afflicting poor areas are the direct result of official policies: "The man wants it that way. He doesn't put any money into the poor areas, so we fight it out and rip each other off." A White, middle-class block club member shares this cynicism:

> I think there are unseen things that are pulling our strings. There are power structures in this country that want to see personal integrity go down the drain.

And in Wicker Park many residents perceive the entire political system as corrupt and believe that the city officials are interested in the real estate, but not the people who live in the area. Neighborhood leaders working to improve their community lack the resources available in other areas. They cannot, like the leaders in Back of the Yards, ascertain the ownership of homes and real estate in the area and, thus, cannot pressure owners to improve dilapidated buildings and neglected vacant lots. They are unable to obtain mortgage money to improve their own homes, and, like the activists in the other two neighborhoods, they share the frustration of a Sunset leader who noted, "If this community could get it together, I know it would be a powerful force."

The residents in Sunset are more economically and educationally advantaged than those in Wicker Park and Mission. They do not confront the serious social or physical maintenance problems prevalent in the other two neighborhoods. Their crime rates are considerably lower. But they do share with the residents of Mission an exceedingly high population turnover. Thirty-three percent of the residents in Mission and 20 percent of those in Sunset have lived in the area one year or less. That may help explain why, along with the residents in the other two sites, they have been unable to develop either the organizational strength or alternative tactics that make it possible to elicit the city services their neighborhoods require. Thus, although the residents in these communities combat problems that differ qualitatively and quantitatively, they share a sense of powerlessness and helplessness as they try to cope with their concerns.

The Moral and Political Order in the Local Community

Although we have discussed the moral and political order as separate dimensions, the two are closely related. The moral order of the community consists of the shared values and norms that enable local residents to predict how their neighbors are likely to behave. Political order is maintained by the agencies of the state. Those most relevant to neighborhood residents are the city service bureaucracies and the police. The former provide neighborhood maintenance support. To a large extent they shape the physical ambiance of the neighborhood, which in turn provides cues indicating whether or not this is a "good" place to live, The police, on the other hand, must influence the behavior of people in the locality who pose a threat to its security. They do this either by deterring criminal and marginally criminal behavior or by apprehending and removing from the neighborhood those who are thus engaged.

The effectiveness with which city services and police protection are delivered seems to reflect in part the political power of neighborhood residents, which appears to have some impact on the rapidity with which population change occurs. Although political power does not seem to be related to individual decisions to move out of a neighborhood, it does appear to be relevant to the maintenance of conditions that prevent massive out-migration. Historically, neighborhoods populated by minority residents who have replaced the White, middle and working class population fleeing to the suburbs have experienced physical deterioration in both residential and commercial areas. And, although the relationship between these two phenomena is unclear and subject to conflicting amd emotionally charged interpretations, it does appear that neighborhoods with some degree of political power have been able to contain both population change and prevent physical decay. The contrast between Back of the Yards and Wicker Pack is a striking illustration of this point.

It is difficult to determine whether the stable population in Back of the Yards and South Philadelphia were maintained because of the individual characteristics of the residents who had no desire to leave the area, or because both neighborhoods were politically powerful enough to control access and to assure adequate maintenance. The combined strength of the moral and political order in these communities makes the relative contribution of each dimension difficult to ascertain.

The history of Lincoln Park, however, illustrates the contribution of political power. The Lincoln Park Conservation Association (LPCA) was organized specifically to exert influence over the direction of change in the area. The gentrification of the neighborhood and the homogeneity of the current population is testimony to its effectiveness in defending the territory.

Thus, local residents with political power appear to be able to influence indirectly the nature and rapidity of population change in their area. Where such change is slow and incremental as in South Philadelphia and Back of the Yards, the dominant values of the community appear to be sustained. And where, as in Lincoln Park, political power was exercised to create an economically homogeneous neighborhood, the maintenance of middle- and upper-middle-class values is assured.

Activists in the more effective organizations in Visitacion Valley, Woodlawn, West Philadelphia, and Logan understand the nexus between the moral and political order. As one Logan leader stated:

> We're saying power comes from our neighbors, our friends from people getting together . . . . We are here to say that the heart and soul of Logan is not in the pocket of self-seeking politicians . . . or in the hands of bankers . . . or the realtors. Power is in our blocks, homes, churches.

This vision of grassroots power provides a clear indication of the changing nature of the urban political order. In the past, political power was exercised by local party operatives and elected officials who served as intermediaries between the citizenry and the municipal service bureaucracies. However, as party organizations grew weaker, community residents began to see government not so much as an agent of the people responsible to the message of the electorate, but rather as a bureaucratic service agency operating outside of the electoral accountability system. The neighborhood movement and the organizations it spawned, therefore, concentrated primarily on the bureaucracy and worked to move the focus of political power from the party to neighborhood grassroots groups. This ideology was clearly illustrated in the comment of one Logan resident when questioned about approaching the Democratic party for help:

> Oh no, we don't do that. We're not supposed to work with them. The whole idea is for the people to get things done.

Thus, where previously the moral order of the local community may have been dependent solely on economic and political forces external to the area, organizational activists in this study suggest that the sustenance of the moral order requires an effective neighborhood-based political order.

7

Crime, Fear and Community Context

In the preceding chapters we have developed an analysis of fear of crime as a problem of social control. Following in the tradition of Park and Burgess (1925), we see this social problem as emerging in situations where community residents appear to be limited in their capacity to regulate people's behavior. Fear of crime then becomes a reaction to a set of circumstances experienced by neighborhood populations. As such it is best understood, we believe, as an aspect of collective action, for it is produced by situations where one is concerned about what others have done, are doing, and may do in the future. When that action indicates a lack of conformity to conventional values (e.g., "thou shalt not steal"), the *moral reliability* of the community disintegrates.

Community environments consist of both physical settings and the people who live their lives within them. Local residents adapt their behavior to both of these environmental components. They do what they do with an eye to what others expect and what they expect from others. Such collective action reflects what people ordinarily take into account concerning what is going on around them and what is likely to go on after they decide what they will do (Becker 1973).

When the "moral reliability" of a community dissolves, local residents are no longer sure that the behavior of their neighbors will conform to what in the past were uniformally acceptable standards, and fear of crime appears. Thus, this fear is produced by situations that engender concern about what others have done, are doing, and may do in the future. Because of the heterogeneity of the population, city life puts a premium on moral reliability. City dwellers learn to distinguish between those they can trust and those they cannot. The trustworthy, those who share our values, serve as the building blocks for our lives, while the untrustworthy are avoided.

Thus, people can be relied on to the extent that they share expectations about each other's behavior and can be disciplined when those expectations are violated. Those people whose behavior is not subject to the moral order are dangerous both because they cannot be relied upon and because they will not accept discipline. Within the urban context, we look for cues from individuals and environments to signal their reliability. We spend a great deal of time creating and maintaining sets of relationships that minimize contact with those who appear unreliable. Therefore, it is not so much the violation of norms that makes us fearful (for that violation is a necessary consequence of their enforcement), but rather that those norms are not shared in the first place. Within any moral order there will be those who live up to common standards better than others (Dahrendorf, 1968). That cannot be avoided. Fear becomes a problem, however, when we cannot assume that common standards shape behavior. Thus, strangers are dangerous until they signal the acceptance of common standards, usually in their dress and demeanor.

Local environments provide the contours for collective action. And although the meaning of these environments and how they are experienced may vary somewhat depending on cultural backgrounds, they are, by and large, public and the adjustments to them are collective. The capacity to shape these environments, however, is not equally distributed. There are significant differences both in the resilience of community conditions and in the ability of local groups to deal with them through concerted action. Indicators of incivility, of available resources, and of the ways they are combined, therefore, differ in specific neighborhood settings. These combinations, we argue, constitute the context in which fear is generated.

Neighborhood residents use both their individual resources and those of local organizations and leaders in an effort to modify situations they perceive to be threatening to the moral order of their communities. The perceived severity of the threats, as well as the adequacy of their resources, determine the effectiveness with which residents can cope, and this in turn may be reflected in the fear of crime in the neighborhood. By looking at the neighborhoods with similar levels of fear, we can clarify further those forces that engender fear and those that appear to generate a sense of security.

The "high fear" neighborhoods differ in visible signs of social disorganization, in concerns expressed by neighborhood residents, and in available resources. Signs of physical deterioration are found throughout Wicker Park and Woodlawn, but are less evident in Visitacion Valley. Racial tension and conflict pose serious problems for residents in Wicker Park and Visitacion Valley, but not for those in predominantly Black Woodlawn.

Teens, drugs, and vandalism concern more residents in Wicker Park than in any of the other sites. Woodlawn comes close to Wicker Park in concern about drugs, but moves down to slightly above the median on concern about teens and vandalism. A considerably smaller percentage of Visitacion Valley residents report that these situations pose problems in their community.

Significant differences in available resources are also evident. Residents in Wicker Park and Woodlawn lack the support provided by moderately high levels of income and education. The population in Visitacion Valley has slightly superior educational and significantly better economic resources. Particularly important in this regard is its higher percentage of homeowners who, at a miminum, have some control over their immediate environment, which is unavailable to those who rent.

All three neighborhoods exhibit a similar moderate ranking on our informal social integration measure, but they differ significantly on the level of involvement in community affairs and the effectiveness of the organizations in their neighborhoods. Wicker Park residents report the lowest level of involvement among all ten sites. Woodlawn and Visitacion Valley rank third and fourth respectively. Although all three neighborhoods have Alinsky-style organizations operating within them, Wicker Park's has been the least effective in generating response and in involving community residents. The organizations in Woodlawn and Visitacion Valley have both achieved a fair measure of visible success. The most active organizations in the latter two neighborhoods adopted a self-help model that encourages active participation in community problem-solving. In Wicker Park, however, relationships with service agencies rather than grass roots organizations are more prevalent. And there the client professional relationship might well reinforce dependency feelings in area residents.

These neighborhoods are similar, however, in the perception of their residents about the severity of crime problems in the area and the failure of the city's service bureaucracies to meet area needs. The crime rates in all three neighborhoods are well above their cities' means. And the people who live in them express the highest level of awareness and concern about the most fear provoking crimes, robbery and assault.

In Table 7 we present a simplified illustration of the context of the "high fear" neighborhoods. We have collapsed several measures to determine a high, low, or moderate ranking for neighborhood problems and resources. The problems on the left side of the table include the incivility indicators excluding crime, reported crime rates, crime awareness, and crime concerns. The resources on the right side

TABLE 7

Social Disorganization Indicators and Neighborhood Resources:
The "High Fear" Neighborhoods

| | Problems | | | | Resources | | | |
	Incivility Concerns	Crime Rates	Victimization and Awareness	Victimization Concern	Income	Education	Home Ownership	Social Integration	Community Involvement
Wicker Park	High	High	High	High	Low	Low	Moderate	Moderate	Low
Woodlawn	High	High	High	High	Low	Low	Low	Moderate	High
Visitacion Valley	Low	High	High	High	Moderate	Low	High	Moderate	High

include income, education, home ownership, social integration, and community involvement.*

This table suggests that there are real differences in the quality of life experienced by the residents in these neighborhoods. On the one hand we have Visitacion Valley, a relatively well-maintained area whose residents express few concerns about the major issues generally confronting residents in high crime areas. Woodlawn and Wicker Park, on the other hand, reflect the urban crisis in its most extreme form. Visitacion Valley residents also have better resources than those in the other two neighborhoods. Inhabitants of Woodlawn also have some advantages. They do not have to deal with racial conflict, and they do have the support provided by a well-established community organization. Furthermore, as we noted earlier, a little over one-third of the residents perceive improvement in their neighborhood.

The residents in all three communities confront high levels of victimization relative to the other neighborhoods in this study and share related concerns about crime. We have argued, however, that because crime directly affects a relatively small segment of the population in even high crime areas, fear is frequently provoked by other signs or disorder that remind local residents of the threats surrounding them. These are closely evident in Woodlawn and Wicker Park, but less so in Visitacion Valley.

If there are in Visitacion Valley fewer reminders of the threats posed by potential criminal activity, why do we find a fear level there approximating that in the other two neighborhoods? Two explanations come to mind. It is possible that there is a threshold (Conklin 1975) beyond which the number of victimizations in an area overwhelm all the forces that might otherwise enhance perceptions of neighborhood security. Or we might find in Visitacion Valley other cues that substitute for the social disorder indicators we have identified as signalling the threats posed by crime in the area.

---

*The following procedures were used to determine the ranking of the variables in the table. For the social disorganization indicators an additive scale was formed by assigning one point to each neighborhood for the indicators discussed in the field notes, and one point to each neighborhood where 30 percent or more of the residents expressed concerns about teenagers, drugs, vandalism and 20 or more percent expressed concern about abandoned buildings. The scores ranged from 0-7. A score of 5-7 was high, 2-3 moderate and 0-1 low. The rankings for victimization awareness, concern, community involvement and social integration were determined by the inspection of the position of each neighborhood on the charts, comparing the sites on each of these variables. The rankings on income, education, home ownership, and reported crime rates were determined by each neighborhood's relation to its city's mean. Those well above the mean were ranked high, those approximating the mean were moderate, and those below the mean were low.

A majority of the residents in the area have installed iron gates as target hardening devices. And although these are not as immediately threatening as illegal drug use or abandoned buildings, they do suggest that there is cause for concern. An extensive crime prevention (SAFE) program undertaken during our data-collection period also offered continual reminders of area crimes. Residents were given neighborhood-specific crime statistics; they were told about a variety of protective strategies; they saw movies depicting criminals in action; and they shared local victimization stories. In addition, they were reminded of the limited protection afforded by police. Kidder, Cohn, and Harvey (1978) found that people who engage in victimization prevention report more fear and less control over crime than those who work with community organizations to prevent crime. Our speculation that fear in Visitacion Valley might be heightened by the SAFE program is consistent with that finding. In any case, we have found that the prevalence of victimizations in the area appears to be the major factor associated with fear in those sites where approximately half of the residents report being afraid to go out on the street in their neighborhoods at night.

The percentage of residents reporting that they feel unsafe clusters within three percentage points in five of our "low fear" neighborhoods. The sixth—South Philadelphia—exhibits the lowest fear level and is removed from the cluster by five percentage points.

Table 8 presents the incivility-resource combinations in the *low fear* neighborhoods. Although none exhibit severe problems, a variety of incivility concerns are found in the two Philadelphia neighborhoods and in Back of the Yards. Crime concerns are more prevalent in Lincoln Park, where burglary is a pervasive problem. Only in Sunset and South Philadelphia does one find minimal concerns about both crime and social disorganization indicators.

South Philadelphia falls at the bottom of the fear measure. But residents in Sunset exhibit fear levels approximating those in Lincoln Park, where crime is much more pervasive, and in the other three neighborhoods, where both crime and incivility stimulate some measure of concern. The problems confronting Sunset residents do not appear to explain this phenomenon. But an examination of the right-hand side of the table suggests that fear in Sunset might be accounted for not by the prevalent problems, but rather by its paucity of community problem-solving resources.

Sunset residents have more than adequate personal resources. They share the relatively high income and educational level of the inhabitants of Lincoln Park and the extensiveness of home ownership found in the Philadelphia neighborhoods. But they lack the support of both the

TABLE 8
Social Disorganization Indicators and Neighborhood Resources:
The "Low Fear" Neighborhoods

	Social Disorganization Indicators			
	Incivility Indicators	Crime Rates	Victimization and Awareness	Victimization Concern
West Philadelphia	Moderate	Moderate	Moderate	Low
Logan	Moderate	Moderate	Moderate	Low
Sunset	Low	Low	Low	Low
Back of Yards	Moderate	Moderate	Moderate	Low
Lincoln Park	Low	High	Moderate	Moderate
South Philadelphia	Low	Low	Low	Moderate

	Resources			
	Income	Education	Home Ownership	Social Integration	Community Involvement
West Philadelphia	Low	Low	High	High	High
Logan	Low	Moderate	High	Moderate	High
Sunset	High	High	High	Low	Low
Back of Yards	Moderate	Low	Moderate	Moderate	Moderate
Lincoln Park	High	High	Low	Low	Moderate
South Philadelphia	Low	Low	High	High	Moderate

informal social integration and the organizational effectiveness of groups that can generate high levels of participation in community affairs. Thus, residents in Sunset have failed to translate their personal resources in a manner that might enhance the community's capacity to generate a response to local demands and to exert a measure of social control. This failure might in part be explained by the recent entry into the neighborhood of large numbers of Asians who, because of language and cultural barriers, engage neither in formal nor informal neighboring activities.

Sunset residents face far fewer problems than those in the other sites, yet they perceive changes threatening the cohesion of the community they know and value. And although these changes appear to be relatively minor compared to those confronting residents elsewhere, the reactions in Sunset may well be aggravated by the perceived helplessness of community residents who try to deal with them. Although residents in the other neighborhoods face more serious problems, they all appear to have some kind of community support system available. Residents in Lincoln Park appear to have both the individual and community level resources to more effectively enable them to cope. There are in the neighborhood active organizations with reasonably good relations with the bureaucratic establishment. And although levels of community involvement are not as high as in the two Philadelphia neighborhoods, the political sophistication of area residents and their extra-community ties strengthen their capacity to generate responses to their needs.

Back of the Yards residents do not have the socioeconomic resources of the Lincoln Park residents, but they do have the support of a really potent community organization. Again, levels of involvement are not as high as in the Philadelphia neighborhoods. However, the strength of the organization lies not so much in the current size of its membership, but rather in its status and the status of the executive director and his ties with the Democratic organization and the city bureaucracy. In South Philadelphia, there are close connections with the political establishment, but more important is the high level of social integration that generates a feeling that "we can take care of our own.

The two other Philadelphia neighborhoods present an alternative model for community problem-solving. Lacking both the economic strengths of Lincoln Park residents and the political power of those in the Back of the Yards and in South Philadelphia, they compensate with extensive organizational involvement as they attempt to address community needs.

Neighborhood activists see their relationship with city government as "an ongoing war that we have and will continue to wage." Although this relationship does not produce the responses available to people who already have political or organizational power, it does work to some extent and, when the situation is not too extreme, appears to develop in the residents a sense of being able to exert some control over events in their neighborhood. Organizations in both Logan and West Philadelphia also focus on organizing at the block club level, which creates both a power base and a neighborhood-level support system.

Whatever the source, all five neighborhoods exhibit a local support system that gives residents a feeling that they can exert some control over the environment in which they live. Some of this support, such as social integration, levels of community involvement, home ownership, and other demographically associated strengths of area residents, are locally based and locally derived. But since most serious neighborhood problems are externally induced, their resolution requires external support.

Although the degree to which urban resources are differentially distributed is a matter of some debate (Lineberry 1977; Jones 1979), our field notes indicate that many urban residents perceive a maldistribution and feel that a neighborhood-level power base is required to secure adequate services from city bureaucracies.

The efforts of neighborhood groups to secure such benefits is an example of interest group politics at the local level. The strategies used to get a bureaucratic response varies according to the political and organizational strength of the residents. And the effectiveness of their efforts, the generally recognized presence in an area of an organization known to be able to elicit a bureaucratic response, might well generate among neighborhood residents a sense that they have the capacity to exert some measure of social control.

Feelings of security are psychological responses to objective conditions and, thus, are generated as much by individual interpretations as well as the conditions themselves. The case of Sunset suggests that neighborhood residents confronting relatively few problems may become fearful if they feel that they cannot deal with whatever changes take place. There appears to be little crime in Sunset and a relatively small percentage of residents are concerned. However, the crime rate in San Francisco is the highest for all three cities in this study. Sunset residents, according to our survey, are most likely to read and recall crime stories in the newspapers. And they believe, however low their rates, that crime is increasing in the area. When these perceptions are coupled with the feeling that neighborhood residents are not capable of generating an adequate response to their demands, fear levels in Sunset become more understandable. They are equal to those in the areas where the problems are more severe because of the perceived helplessness of the residents who feel that they cannot adequately respond to any difficulties they confront.

Skogan (1980) has argued that Black and low-income populations are more fearful because they are "socially" vulnerable. This social vulnerability reflects the fact that those on the lower end of the socioeconomic status scale are frequently unable to generate the resources that make up a secure environment. We argue that communities can also be viewed as vulnerable if the activists experience repeated failure in their efforts to secure a response from city bureaucratic and political agencies. Cohen (1979) has classified neighborhoods according to the political capacities generated by community groups. By his standards, the three low-income neighborhoods in Philadelphia are more politically advantaged than Sunset, which is viewed by its activists as politically deprived and therefore, vulnerable. Our analysis of Sunset is particularly instructive because it is a deviant case that defies our expectations about the relationship of socioeconomic status and political power. It is cases such as this, however, that clarify forces that might otherwise be submerged in the expected association of status and power.

What have we learned here about the relationship of fear and neighborhood context? Our analysis of the high fear neighborhoods seems to suggest that there is a threshold beyond which a high incidence of crime in a neighborhood generates a high level of fear regardless of other factors. Differences in community resources appear to have little impact when crime rates and concerns are high. In neighborhoods with a moderate or low level of crime, however, community resources may make a difference. This is particularly true of community organizations that generate an active commitment to the area. This study suggests that where local residents lack political power, effective organizations can compensate. And it suggests that where neighborhood residents perceive that they are receiving inadequate support from city bureaucracies and are unable to generate community involvement and organizational strength, political alienation and a sense of helplessness are more likely to be generated. Whether such neighborhoods face extremely severe problems, such as those in Wicker Park, moderately severe problems, such as those in Mission, or minor problems, such as those in Sunset, the message to the residents is clear: They do not have the capacity to control the changes that are threatening the quality of life in their neighborhoods. This perceived lack of control might well engender as much fear as the threatening situations themselves.

This interpretation should not be minimized by its relevance primarily to our low fear neighborhoods; the fact that a little more than one-fourth of the residents in these sites exhibit fear suggests that this constitutes a problem demanding serious attention. Indeed, it is more likely that fear reduction policies would be more effective in such neighborhoods than in those like Wicker Park and Woodlawn, where the severe social problems themselves, rather than the fear they generate, should be directly addressed.

8

Social Problems, Public Policy and Political Responsibility

Gusfield (1975) has made the useful distinction between the *cognitive* and *political* responsibility for a social problem. By the former, he means explaining why the problem occurs and by the latter, who is obliged to solve it. We have developed our own public position on the cognitive responsibility for fear of crime and proposed it in contradistinction to the prevailing explanation for the problem. We then examined the fear of crime in ten communities from the social control perspective, trying to persuade the reader that our explanation might help account for the distribution of the social problem under discussion.

In this chapter we turn our attention to the question of political responsibility and to the relationship between the cognitive and political dimensions. Gusfield points out that there is no necessary logical link between the cognitive and political dimensions, that is, a problem may be caused by factors that are independent of the political responsibility for its solution (e.g., inflation and the federal government responsibility). We will argue, however, that in the case of fear of crime, the link between the cognitive and political dimensions is made by the various criminal justice interest groups that tie the two dimensions together in theory as well as practice. The cognitive and political dimensions are produced by actors whose values and interests link the two spheres. Since there is a high value placed on rationality in social reform, these connections are presented logically, each position supporting the other's claim to legitimacy. The cognitive dimension often explicitly, and sometimes implicitly, contains the suggestion of where the political responsibility for the problem ought to be located. The interest groups that, at any given time, either hold, or seek to hold this political responsibility will be selective in promoting the construction of problems that strengthen their claim. These interest groups are likely to present particular pictures of cognitive and political responsibility that benefit themselves.

111

We are speaking here of the "competing public position," not the almost infinite variety of private opinions, personal preferences, and academic musings that surround the social problem debate. These "positions" are put forth in public and taken seriously by others; they shape how elites think about the issues and what they propose to do about them. While the origins of the cognitive aspects of the problem can be manifold, the extent to which that approach emerges in public discussion depends upon the uses to which these aspects can be put by the interest groups who seek to control both the policy agenda and arena. Indeed, the policy that develops from various approaches to social problems is not a "natural" consequence of objective investigation, but rather an ideological tool in the hands of those who seek control over the remedies to the problem.

We see three major interests groups with competing public positions on the fear of crime issue. Those groups are loose-knit associations of individuals who represent the "structural interests" in criminal justice. Our typology borrows heavily from Alford's (1975) analysis of health care policy, where the alignment of interests is much the same. He identifies three groups that represent the structural interests in the health care arena—the professional monopolists, the corporate rationalizers, and the "equal health advocates." The monopolists argue for leaving the decision to professionals (mostly doctors) and the marketplace, and the rationalizers seek to regulate both doctors and markets to distribute health care more "rationally." There is much accommodation and compromise between these groups, which leaves the basic economic, professional, and political relationships among the interest groups intact, but may shift power relations marginally between the competing actors. Equal health advocates often criticize the reliance on the market system in health care, but have had little success in challenging its dominance. They represent lower-class groups who are the least competitive in the marketplace.

The criminal justice system and the health care system may be seen as parallel systems. Both distribute a value as a supplement to the market systems. The availability of health and security services, in the main, is a function of one's position in the class system. While members of the upper classes can become seriously ill and experience serious victimization, their class position makes available optimum resources that help them maintain security and health. Indeed, two of the main benefits of upward mobility are increased health and safety. The two *care* systems (medical and criminal justice) supplement those market relations and the distribution that follows from them. Both are *reactive*, responding to individual requests for service when a health or safety deficiency is reported. Both systems declare themselves to be *in crisis* regularly, particularly around the issue of how they distribute their services. And both "solve" those crises by bringing representatives of the interest groups together. The three criminal justice groups paralleling those defined by Alford in the health care field include the police, courts, and corrections personnel who make up the professional monopolists; the more recent created criminal justice coordinating agencies, such as the Federal Law Enforcement Assistance Administration, who make up the rationalizers; and the equal security advocates represented primarily by grass roots community groups. Each of these groups has an explicit solution to the crime and fear problem, which is based on an implicit analysis. The monopolists seek to pump more resources into the institutions they represent. The rationalizers look to coordination and planning to improve the services and the bargaining position of the institutions they represent. And the equal security advocates, among whom we count ourselves, see the solution in community empowerment.

Each of these groups developed a public position on both the cognitive and political responsibility for fear of crime. In the discussion that follows, we will concentrate on the positions of the rationalizers and monopolists, leaving the equal security position to be developed in the final chapter.

The victimization perspective played an important role in surfacing the fear problem and in assigning the cognitive responsibility for fear upon the experience of the victimization event and the individual reaction to it.

John Conklin made this important connection between event and individual response in *The Impact of Crime* (1975). Rejecting Emile Durkheim's concept of the functionality of deviance in strengthening communities, Conklin argues that fear of crime robs citizens of the capacity to trust, isolates them, and thus contributes to the decline of community.

> Little of the material we have examined . . . suggests that Durkheim was correct in arguing that crime brings people together and strengthens social bonds. Instead, crime produces insecurity, distrust, and a negative view of the community. Although we lack conclusive evidence, crime also seems to reduce social interaction as fear and suspicion drive people apart. This produces a disorganized community that is unable to exercise informal social control over deviant behavior.

This scenario is predicated on the notion that people react to crime as individuals. Rather than collectively sanctioning the criminal behavior, as Durkheim would anticipate, citizens react individually to fear and seek to protect themselves (e.g., buying guns and locks, not going out), thus breaking community cohesion.

Conklin's discussion of community hinges on the distinction he makes between *individual* and *collective* responses to crime. The importance of these responses in turn stems from Conklin's use of the victimization perspective, for the logic of responding individually hinges on the salience of the victimization experience. Individual responses are assumed to be the normal reaction to the fear, or experience, of victimization. Thus, the conclusion that individual responses have negative consequences hinges on the imputed salience of victimization. Interestingly enough, this line of reasoning makes the *response* to victimization, rather than victimization itself, the central phenomenon. Conklin goes on to argue that when a community can respond collectively, crime does integrate:

> Crime weakens the fabric of social life by increasing fear, suspicion, and distrust. It also reduces public support for the law, in terms of unwilling-ness to report crime and criticism of the police. However, under certain conditions people will engage in collective action to fight crime. They may work for a political candidate who promises to restore law and order. They may call meetings of community residents to plan an attack on crime. Sometimes they may even band together in a civilian police patrol to carry out the functions that the police are not effectively performing for them. Since people who perceive high crime rates often hold the police responsible for crime prevention, we would expect such patrols to emerge where people feel very threatened by crime, believe that the police cannot protect them, and think from past experience with community groups that the people themselves can solve the problem.

Whether or not the response is individual or collective, the cognitive responsibility for the production of fear rests with the victimization event. The political responsibility, however, is determined by the kind of response a community produces. The rationalizers develop crime prevention strategies encouraging collective responses to deter crime and reduce fear. They seek to reduce the number of victimizations in a neighborhood by increasing the capacity of the community to respond collectively. The monopolists assume that the response will be individual and that police must be responsible for reducing both crime and the fear that it engenders.

Figure 12 schematizes the previous discussion of cognitive responsibility. Fear of crime is "caused" by the sequence depicted on the *high road* in the figure. Victimization leads to fear. The political responsibil-

FIGURE 12
Victimization Perspective

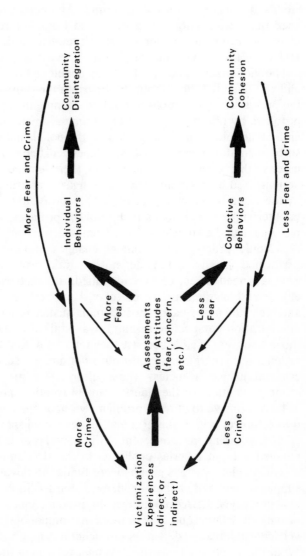

ity is not given in the sequence and depends on how one interprets cognitive responsibility.

The policy issue can be put succinctly: who has the political responsibility for dealing with fear of crime? The bureaucratic rationalizers used the victimization perspective and Conklin's refinement of it to claim the problem for themselves. Several federal agencies (LEAA, HUD, ACTION) have mounted crime prevention programs.

The victimization perspective was developed during the late 1960s and was nurtured throughout the 1970s. In the simplest terms, it broke the professional monopolists' hold on defining the magnitude of crime problem, by offering a picture of a crime problem that was politically and methodologically independent of the police and courts. However, since the rationalizers at LEAA depended upon the monoplists for much of their support at budget times, their demands for reform had to be tempered by restraint. The "dark figure" of crime was illuminated by the victimization perspective, but, in a way, to create a supplemental alternative rather than a picture of the problem. This supplemental picture created a knowledge base from which criminal justice rationalizers could propose management changes in how the monopolists performed their jobs. In order not to strain relations too much, new groups in need of service were identified. Among these groups were the elderly and middle class, resentful of the poverty programs of the past and presently unserved by most criminal justice programs. Much of the victimization perspective research was utilized to expand services to those who were eligible because they felt afraid. Reducing fear of crime rationalized programming for groups not directly served by traditional criminal justice agencies. These efforts (victim-witness programs, crime prevention for the elderly, rape prevention, and so on appeared to be responsive to current problems without challenging the distribution of power within the criminal justice establishment. Just like the community relations movement of the previous decade, a "crisis" was handled without a series challenge to the structural interests of key constituencies. Various groups were funded to develop programs that supplemented, rather than challenged, the traditional criminal justice constituencies. LEAA could thereby produce innovation without disturbing the status quo and professional monopolists found that they needed "innovations" to secure federal support for local efforts. Within local jurisdictions, professional reformers (local corporate rationalizers) could demand new programs that appeared to be alternatives, but were in fact supplemental in function.

In this respect LEAA behaves no differently than other federal agencies. This agency had the difficult charge of changing a system on which it depended for its very existence. Thus, the actions of the agency had to have the appearance of altering the status quo, while being acceptable to the central constituencies. This leads to what Wilson (1975) has called *criminal justice syndicalism:* "the tendency for decisions to be unduly influenced by the organized interests of those whose behavior is to be changed." Consequently, there was a high premium on programs and policies that seemed to change, but which, in fact, enhanced the position and authority of the institutions to be reformed. The rationalizers simply expanded the service field to allow new programs to be established without upsetting the status quo. A few examples should illustrate this point.

The program guidelines go even further in outlining the type of efforts that will be funded:

> Priority will be given to programs and activities that are public minded in the sense that they are designed to promote a social or collective response to crime and the fear of crime at the neighborhood level in contrast to "private minded" efforts that deal only with the actions of citizens as individuals or those that result from the provision of services that in themselves do not contribute to the organization of the neighborhood. [U.S. Department of Justice 1977:58-3]

Victimization experiences are assumed to create fear. Fear in turn generates isolation, because citizens react individually to the threat. Crime consequently disintegrates community. Criminal occurrences and fear can be reduced if citizens react collectively to that threat. The CACP guidelines are quite explicit about the program's goal:

> To encourage neighborhood anti-crime efforts that promote a greater sense of community and foster social controls over crime occurrence. [U.S. Department of Justice 1977:58-1]

Crime events are seen as promoting the decline of community, and federally funded collective action to prevent those events is seen as the solution to the fear problem.

Interestingly, in both these cases the political responsibility for controlling the problem is diffused. If the problematic situation is fear of crime, then it is not clear who is charged with stimulating the collective response. While a variety of agencies have funded these efforts, the actual intervention is often left to the local agencies and groups receiving the aid. The community organization is obliged to solve the problem, usually in cooperation with other agencies both public and private. These solutions were only temporary since they depended upon categorical grants and the approval of local officials and, while useful innovations from LEAA perspective, offered no lasting challenge to the monopolists.

The Hartford Crime Prevention Program was one of the first federally funded efforts. The rationale of the Hartford Crime Prevention Program (a federally funded demonstration project) is as follows:

1. The crime rate in a residential neighborhood is a product of the linkage between offender motivation and the opportunities provided by the residents, users, and environmental features of that neighborhood.
2. The crime rate for a specific offense can be reduced by lessening the opportunities for that crime to occur.
3. Opportunities can be reduced by (a) altering the physical aspects of buildings and streets to increase surveillance capabilities and lessen target/victim vulnerability, to increase the neighborhood's attractiveness to residents, and to decrease its fear-producing features; (b) increasing citizens concerns about the involvement in crime prevention and the neighborhood in general; and (c) utilizing the police to support the above.
4. Opportunity-reducing activities will lead not only to a reduction in the crime rate but also to a reduction in fear of crime. The reduced crime and fear will mutually reinforce each other, leading to still further reductions in both. [Fowler et al. 1979:2]

The Hartford approach sets in motion a series of interventions that literally reshaped the targeted community, and, if they are successful, will reshape the potential vulnerability of citizens to victimization. While this approach indirectly affects the motivation of offenders by increasing their risk of apprehension and decreasing the benefits to be obtained through illegal activities, the emphasis has shifted away from changing their personalities or economic opportunities. The traditional criminological theories of crime causation emphasized socialization, subcultural and class variables, and attempted prevention strategies that manipulated these factors. Here we find no mention of class, norms, or human development. Rather, a utilitarian, rationalistic approach dominates, which aims at reshaping social relations among residents. Motivation still remains central, but it is the motivation of the offended rather than the offender that becomes pivotal to the success of the intervention. Individuals must be *motivated* to act collectively rather than individually. Organizations are developed to give individuals options when they respond to crime. The success of this program as described by its evaluators lay in its reduction of fear and distrust, rather than a significant decline in crime.

The Community Anti-Crime Program (CACP) offers a slightly different approach to utilizing the victimization perspective in a crime and fear reduction strategy. Introduced in the summer of 1977, and sponsored by LEAA, the CACP was authorized to spend 30 million dollars in direct grants to community organizations:

> To assist community organizations, neighborhood groups and individual citizens in becoming actively involved in activities designed to prevent crime, reduce the fear of crime and improve the administration of justice. [U.S. Department of Justice 1977:58]

The program's guidelines also describe the problems that the grants are meant to alleviate:

> The increasing social isolation of neighborhood residents, resulting from a fear of crime, which has destroyed the feelings of community necessary for social control. [U.S. Department of Justice 1977:58]

And the program guidelines are equally clear about what types of activities the program is meant to foster:

> The mobilization of community and neighborhood residents into effective self-help organizations to conduct anti-crime programs within their communities and neighborhoods. To encourage neighborhood anti-crime efforts that promote a greater sense of community and foster social controls over crime occurrence. [U.S. Department of Justice 1977:58-1]

Community organizations have neither the political muscle nor the formal authority to monopolize the "ownership" of the fear problem (Gusfield 1975). Thus, their early success in assuming the political responsibility for the problem lay in the benefits to the sponsoring federal agencies.

The policy of increasing the likelihood of collective responses served the rationalizers well. Rather than attempting to alter the predispositions and motivations of the criminal, as progressive reforms throughout the century had sought to do, rationalizers sought to prevent crime and reduce fear by altering the relations between the criminal, victim, and environment, thereby reducing the opportunity for victimization. Crime is to be prevented and fear reduced not by changing perpetrators, but rather by educating potential victims, limiting the opportunities for victimization, and thus reducing fear. This was an innovation. For the first time in this century, a crime prevention policy has emerged that aims at changing the behavior of community residents and the structure of urban communities, not because they produce criminals, but rather because they produce victims.

In the past, the crime problem belonged to the criminal. The cognitive responsibility lay either with the criminal or the environment that produced him, while the political responsibility lay with criminal justice agencies. The Community crime prevention, as we call the rationalizers' approach, gave the cognitive responsibility to the victim and his environment, and the political responsibility to the *collective response* of community groups. But this attributing of political responsibility to community groups came in a context that demanded no change in the control of criminal justice decision making, in exchange for the responsiblity to control the problem.

If we can thank the corporate rationalizers at LEAA for the emergence of community crime prevention, we should also expect that the other "structural interests" involved would develop competing public positions on the issue of fear of crime. To fail to do so, or to deny that fear is a problem, would leave the field to the one public position supported by the federal bureaucrats.

Perhaps the most important competing position comes from the professional monopolists who have redefined both the cognitive and political responsibility for the problem. The clearest and most important articulation of this position comes from Wilson and Kelling in *Broken Windows* (1982). They argue that fear of crime can be reduced through policing practice. Their approach hinges on the elaboration of the *high road* sketched in Figure 12. They focus in particular on the way community disintegration affects the production of crime, and they suggest that police patrolling strategies can mitigate that production process by forestalling the disintegration process.

> The citizen who fears the ill-smelling drunk, the rowdy teenager, or the importuning beggar is not merely expressing his distaste for unseemly behavior, he is also giving voice to a bit of folk wisdom that happens to be a correct generalization—namely that serious street crime flourishes in areas in which disorderly behavior goes unchecked. The unchecked panhandler is, in effect, the first broken window. Muggers and robbers, whether opportunistic or professional, believe they reduce their chances of being caught or even identified if they operate on streets where potential victims are already intimidated by prevailing conditions. If the neighborhood cannot keep a bothersome panhandler from annoying a passerby, the thief may reason, it is even less likely to call the police to identify a potential mugger or to interfere if the mugging actually takes place. [Wilson and Kelling 1982:34]

By policing against *incivilities,* crime and fear can be curtailed. There are two important points about this approach. First, it assumes the victimization perspective, but suggests that successful intervention pivots less on how individuals react to crime and more on influencing the conditions that produce the crime. Implicitly they believe that crime produces fear and that if crime is curtailed fear will be too. The connection between disorderly behavior, crime, and fear is asserted. In this scenario, it is only the *coercive* power of the police that has the potential to curb disorderly behavior. "The police are plainly the key to order maintenance" [Wilson and Kelling 1982:36]. This is the case because they are the only group that can force an end to disorderly behavior stimulating criminality. This brings us to the second point, solving the fear problem rests with traditional criminal justice agencies. Through this analysis the professional monoplists can reassert their ownership of the fear issue. Informal social control may be the key to maintaining order, but the police are alone in being able to affect directly the behavior that challenges that order. Thus, fear of crime can be lessened to the extent that disorderly behavior is reduced. Community organizations have little capacity to reduce the incidence of disorderly behavior. Police can solve the problem through changes in their practices. The cause of the disorderly behavior does not have to be addressed in its solution. Coercion can go a long way in reducing crime and fear, especially if the coercion supports the conventional standards of the community.

Equal security advocates place the cognitive responsibility for the problem in the lack of social control in some communities. To ameliorate the fear problem, that control must be reasserted. Community organizations are the appropriate vehicles for this solution, given their capacity to enforce neighborhood standards. If the community is *empowered* through its local organizations to assert that control, fear will be reduced.

Each position has a different notion of the "motor" for social control. That is, the reduction of fear follows from the process each interest group puts into action through its analyses and strategies. The professional monopolists rely on *coercion,* the corporate rationalizers on bureaucratic *cooperation,* and the equal security advocates on *empowerment.* There are three competing positions, each of which offers a vision of how fear might be reduced, and each of which serves the interests of a constituency in the criminal justice arena. Those interests are served by suggesting that the problem can be ameliorated by placing the issue in the hands of one of the constituencies.

While the professional monopolists and corporate rationalizers rely on the victimization perspective in their assessments of cognitive responsibility, we have returned to the social control perspective to create a competing position on fear of crime. In the next section, we will compare these positions more directly and, through that comparison, determine which position best accounts for the distribution of fear of crime.

9

Fear of Crime and Political Responsibility

In this chapter, we will discuss how the contemporary social control perspective shapes an agenda of political responsibility for equal security advocates. By describing how cognitive and political responsibility interact in our own work and comparing that approach to the other contending positions, we hope to persuade the reader of the viability of our perspective as both an explanation of the fear of crime phenomenon and a prescription for how to *treat* the problem. We will argue that lack of social control triggers fear and the introduction of that control, that is, the power to regulate the behavior of others, will decrease it. The responsibility for introducing that control lies with groups of residents who seek to have their values and interests protected.

Thus, the political responsibility for the problem of fear is logically contained within the cognitive responsibility for its emergence. The work of Suttles and Janowitz provide the link between the two dimensions by emphasizing the practical, self-interested aspects of standard setting and deemphasizing the assumption of value integration as a precondition for group activity. Community residents are assumed to be self-interested. Assessing their needs for security, safety, and independence in terms of the community's resources, citizens act in the local context to achieve these values. These practical decisions and behaviors create an environment that *limits liability* and regulates behavior. They create a viable order, not out of a value consensus, but out of the process of negotiating a relatively secure environment. These are practical down-to-earth matters and involve thousands of warnings, stories, and experiences through which compromises, truces, and settlements are reached between those who must live and work in proximity. Thus, social control is not a consequence of shared values, rather, social control is the process of sharing that which is valued. Competition between groups and individuals for scarce resources constitutes the building blocks of social order. Suttles argues that these negotiations build community, not as primordial attachment of individuals to a territorial group, but as the accommodation of *proximate strangers* (Keller 1968) to each other. That is, what happens between groups is more important than what happens within them:

> The defended neighborhood is primarily a response to fears of invasion from adjacent community areas. It exists, then, with a structure of parallel residential solidarities which stand in mutual opposition. And it is this mutual opposition rather than primordial solidarity alone which gives the defended neighborhood its unity and sense of homogeneity. [Suttles 1968:58]

Our formulation of the social control perspective modifies the analysis of the Chicago School in two substantial ways. First, it rejects the notion that a reproduction of a value concensus can effectively serve as an instrument of social control. And second, it looks to secondary rather than primary institutions to modify the environment so that the exercise of social control is again feasible.

Our investigation identified several neighborhoods where residents maintained or recreated a value consensus by using political power to keep "undesirables" out of the area. Aside from the ethical questions that might be raised about such strategies, they are clearly not applicable in a society characterized by increasing socioeconomic, racial, and ethnic heterogeneity. In addition, as Granovetter (1973) and others have discussed, *residential solidarities* can be a mixed blessing in opposing invasion. Often, tightly-knit ethnic cliques are incapable of concerted action to combat problems (Gans 1962). They lack the weak ties between cliques that would stimulate community organizations to battle major threats (e.g., urban renewal, highways, and so on) to the entire area. The key to developing these weak ties may be structural (local voluntary associations, local employment options) or idiosyncratic (strong leadership, outside organizers, and so forth), but without them collective action is most difficult even in the most homogeneous community.

The implication is that reproducing value consensus and value integration to reduce fear of crime may be misguided, even if it were possible. Social control may be negotiated best by those drawn together by self-interest rather than common norms.

The reliance on primary institutions has run into serious problems as well. These problems became clear when the Chicago School's social control perspective was applied during the early years of the Chicago Area Project. Saul Alinsky was employed by the project in these early years, but was drawn away from delinquency prevention toward a more radical community organizing approach by the labor union activities around the stock yards. Alinsky had been assigned to a community adjacent to Back of the Yards, but went to Back of the Yards to play a pivotal role starting the Back of the Yards Council, an organization we discussed earlier. Alinsky applied union organizing tactics to the basic model of the Chicago Area Project. If business and industry were causing social disorganization by these activities, then business and industry ought to be made to change their ways. Communities could not regulate themselves without exerting some control over the organizations undermining community life. Thus, while John L. Lewis' Coal Miners Union helped unionize the stock yards, Alinsky assembled a coalition of union, church, and community leaders to build an organization to improve community life. Using tactics from labor organizing, community organizations challenged business and government to serve the residents better.

While Alinksy-style organizing has run into its own set of theoretical and practical difficulties, his early defection from the Chicago Area Project highlights some of the problems of the social control perspective in action. As Finestone (1976) points out in his intelligent discussion of the dilemma, the emphasis on primary group relations as a remedy to delinquency problems overestimated the curative power of primary institutions. The optimistic action that local adult intervention into the world of adolescence would inculcate conventional values was undermined by the resilience of delinquency in poor communities. The hope that communities could overcome the disorganizing influence of city life was dampened by the significance of social stratification both within the community and as a metropolitan force. The importance of class and the resilience of peer groups was overshadowing the issues of community and urban process in the world of preventing delinquency. The issue of class as both a *structure* that is not so easily changed in the wider society and a divisive *force* within the local community cannot be dismissed by a recognition of common values. Indeed, either that very value consensus makes the distribution of resources a serious problem for those who have not achieved those values, or the lack of a consensus makes the hegemony of certain values oppressive to those who do not share them. The history of social control efforts gives vivid testimony to the pitfalls of preventing crime and delinquency by attempting to socialize the young and regulate their behavior through primary relationships.

As a basis for the equal security advocacy position, we thus offer a reconceptualization of social control, which we see as a liability-limiting process premised on the pursuit of order and security. It is a process of exerting authority over the way individuals and groups interact, not on a foundation of common values, but rather on a basis of common concerns. The *process* of regulating the behavior of others may be as important for social control as the value consensus of the residents of the community. For, while shared values may be a useful foundation for exerting social control, the shared practice of coping with problems may better generate orderly relations between conflicting groups. Communities in which values are shared may not be able to meet the challenge of *invasion,* while communities with weak ties may be able to control disruptive activities. The key to the capacity to exert social control lies in the mechanisms developed within and between groups for the purpose of reducing conflict and enhancing local authority.

The equal security advocates emphasize the ability of local community institutions to maintain social control. We have seen how powerful community groups can lessen fear levels (Back of the Yards), and how the lack of political and social development can increase fear (e.g., Wicker Park and Sunset). Just as with the Community Action Programs, spawned by President Johnson's War on Poverty, our approach to fear reduction emphasizes the importance of local groups of citizens acting collectively. Fear reduction, from this perspective, results from the political mobilization of local citizens. Formulating the problem this way circumvents the entire criminal justice system in favor of these geographically based, for the most part, citizen-oriented, voluntary associations. This strategy alone has substantial impact on the distribution of resources (Levi and Lipsky 1972). Citizen groups enter the policy arena not as advisors in an ancillary position to the professionals, but as the formulators and implementors of policy. The *authority* to administer public programs may be passed to local groups (Bell and Held 1968). Greenstone and Peterson (1976:XVI) highlight the importance of this point in their discussion of OEO (Office of Equal Opportunity).

> The content of the community action controversy involved a critical issue of political authority: namely, which interests should participate in and be deferred to in the course of framing public policy.

We argue the importance of this approach on the basis of the analyses we have done of ten separate communities. Communities have the potential for reducing fear when local organizations are active in controlling the signs of disorganization. Fear reduction is not simply a matter for the professional. It has, we argue, an added *political* dimension, since it is necessary to mobilize community groups and local leaders who can articulate groups' interests and implement programs themselves (Greenstone and Peterson 1973). The significance of this authority shift from professionals to citizens is substantial, for fear reduction, according to the social control perspective, calls for assisting communities in their efforts to reduce signs of disorganization rather than attempting to reduce victimization through the traditional criminal justice methods (Washnis 1976). This important shift in emphasis places community organizations in a central position, for they serve as both sociological units of analysis and political agents of change. Knowledge of the community and legitimacy within it becomes essential to achieving fear reduction; a perspective that places both the problem and the solution in a community context, gives meaning to the emphasis on local leaders, and dilutes local officials' claims to a professional monopoly on the knowledge necessary to reduce fear.

The equal security advocates can be distinguished from the other two groups by the way they handle social conflict and political competition in concrete situations. The victimization perspective psychologizes these issues, treating them as problems of perception and individual vulnerability. Fear of crime results from how individuals respond to environmental stress brought on by victimizations. Professional monopolists assume the existence of conflict and competition and treat them as a given that must be controlled by the police. Rationalizers transform these issues into technical problems of management and planning, hoping to moderate their influence through a process of cooptation. For they must develop political responsibility for fear of crime in a way that minimizes both the recognition of the conflict between groups and communities, and the political power element involved in reducing fear. They must do this by justifying their own involvement with the issue at the national level and the applicability of solutions to a multiplicity of jurisdictions. Thus, strategies that emphasize the universality of the problem and technical, as opposed to political, analysis will be preferred.

Equal security advocates project conflict and competition to the center of their analysis, seeking to transform the relations between superordinates and subordinates by challenging their legitimacy. They offer an approach that explicitly recognizes conflict and political competition and sees them as the mortar that creates order in urban communities.

Each of the three groups introduce interventions seeking increases in social control. And implicit in these interventions is an analysis that pinpoints the cognitive responsibility for the fear of crime.

According to the victimization perspective, a crime is an event defined by criminal statutes as illegal, which represents a common experience for offender and victim. Fear is a consequence of either direct or indirect experience with the crime event. Persons respond to these events either individually or collectively. Individual responses, because they focus on individual protection, tend to lead to isolation, distrust, and thus deterioration of the community; collective responses, on the other hand, are efforts to decrease crime in the community, induce cohesion, and reduce the opportunities for victimizations to occur. Monopolists seek to reduce the negative impact of individual responses by innovations in policing.

Such innovations, however, have been shown to have the most limited impact in those communities needing the most help. Effective policing requires citizen support and cooperation. Yet such support is least likely to be found in heterogeneous communities with high crime rates, where values are in conflict and alienated residents are more likely to believe that the dominant values in our society do not take their interests or needs into account. Although police can serve as agents for social control, they cannot, by their very nature, be the only source of social control in a community.

Criminal justice rationalizers advocate the use of collective action to manipulate the physical and social context in which the offender operates and, thus, change his motivation. Implicit in this analysis is the notion that a community destroyed by fear of crime can be rebuilt by community organizations.

However, Ellis (1971) and Wrong (1961) suggest that since value consensus is assumed in motivational theories of the social order, these theories cannot account for the *emergence* of that order when consensus has broken down. Once fear of crime erodes the sense of community an individual has developed, the victimization perspective does not provide a method for explaining how fear would lessen. One has learned to be afraid. There is no process specified for learning to feel secure. Collective or police action is called for, but no scheme is developed to demonstrate sociologically or politically why that action should be successful. The victimization perspective shares with the Parsonian consensus theory an inability to explain social order when and where that order is not already operational. Once the individual is motivated to be afraid, the perspective cannot explain the reemergence of the social order that fear destroys. Either the impetus for fear (victimizations) must be removed, or the victimized individual must process victimization information differently. Thus, the fearful individual must change if fear is to be overcome, but why this should happen given his circumstances and proclivities is not explained. Indeed, research indicates that fear of crime is clearly inadequate as a stimulant for community organization.

Aaron Podolefsky and Frederic Dubow's analysis of collective responses to crime found that citizens were not likely to respond to inducements offered by independent crime prevention programs. Participation in crime prevention programs was more likely when programs were sponsored by an organization with mutiple purposes and with which neighborhood residents were already associated. Because a large percentage of members of such organizations participate in crime prevention programs when they are adopted, success in crime prevention appears more likely when the program is aimed at organizations rather than at individuals. However, it was also found that crime serves only infrequently as an organizing impetus for neighborhood groups. Rather, such groups tend to unite around other issues and only take on crime and other social problems when they have achieved some organizational maturity.

Furthermore, there is no systematic evidence that an individual's attitude toward crime is associated with participation in collective responses. Paul Lavrakas (1980) and his coauthors found no relationship between perceptions of crime in the neighborhood and collective participation in crime prevention activities, nor did Podolefsky and Dubow (1981) find a connection between crime concerns and such participation. Communities with higher concerns about burglary, for example, do not exhibit a higher incidence of burglary prevention programs. Instead, participation in crime prevention appears to be more closely associated with membership in community organizations with diverse purposes. Such involvement is not so much associated with attitudes toward crime as it is a function of the community's social composition (family income, number of children, and family status).

Crime prevention programming within the social control perspective of the Chicago School aimed at changing the behavior of potential offenders. Crime prevention programming within the victimization perspective has aimed at changing the behavior of potential victims. Neither perspective has led to policies with much demonstrable success in preventing crime or reducing fear.

The contemporary social control perspective on which the equal security advocacy position is based treats crime as an indicator of increased social disorganization, reflecting a community's incapacity to exert social control. Fear is a response induced by the signs of social disorganization perceived in the environment. Local institutions rather than individuals respond to crime in efforts designed to increase political and social control in the community and to promote social integration among residents. Equal security advocates seek realignment in policy through the use of empowerment strategies.

As we see it, a fear reduction policy, like a poverty reduction strategy, attempts to redistribute a value, in this case security. As such, it must be responsive to the diversity of circumstances and concerns characterizing each locality. Our examination of fear of crime in ten neighborhoods in Chicago, San Francisco, and Philadelphia revealed a broad range of concerns that included, but were not limited to, the crime considered by those working within the victimization perspective. Respondents questioned about crime problems described a range of what we have labeled *incivilities* as undesirable features of their communities—abandoned buildings, teenagers hanging around, illegal drug use, and vandalism. In most instances, these other problems appeared to generate at least as much concern as did the crimes customarily considered by scholars examining fear of crime.

Furthermore, when asked what they were doing about crime in their neighborhoods, respondents listed a wide range of activities that went well beyond those offered by the crime prevention programs envisioned by criminal justice officials. Whereas law enforcement officials identify primarily those activities designed to diminish opportunities for victimization to occur, citizens include in their definition of crime prevention efforts to improve the neighborhood, to promote social integration, and to provide services for young people (Podolefsky and DuBow 1980). Local residents see physical, social, and service improvements in their neighborhoods as effective crime prevention interventions. They recognize, as the victimization orientation does not, the importance of a wide variety of community factors in their attempts to reduce criminal activity.

We also discovered that the levels of fear in some neighborhoods clearly defied expectations that high versus low levels of crime inevitably induce high versus low levels of fear. In seeking to account for such deviations, we again turned to contextual variables; we found that the community's political and social resources appeared to constitute a major mediating force between the perception of crime and other neighborhood problems and the subsequent expression of fear. Neighborhoods with political power, for example, appeared more capable of addressing local problems than did those without it; this capacity often appeared to contribute to diminishing levels of fear.

The power to react to community problems was either derived from well-established political connections or stemmed from the efforts of active community organizations. Neighborhoods without such power, even those where only minimal problems were identified as cause for concern, exhibited fear levels that appeared to be higher than warranted by the crime rate and perceived problems. Fear appeared to be related to the perception of change in the area, especially when local residents had little capacity to control that change.

There were important structural factors that served as additional means of support for local residents confronting crime and related problems. High levels of social integration in neighborhoods were related to lower levels of fear. This could be induced intentionally, via such organizations as block clubs, or develop "naturally" where population movement was minimal and patterns of association within the neighborhood were well established.

Thus, both in the identification of forces that mediate between fear-producing conditions and subsequent expressions of fear, and in community residents' conception of crime problems and appropriate crime prevention activities, the neighborhood context assumes an importance that is overlooked by the research informed by the victimization perspective.

Developing local leadership, strengthening indigenous organizations, and building linkages to government agencies impinging on the community should all be encouraged on the basis of our study. However, this should be done within the context of local definitions of problems and the unique and often complex combinations of factors effecting the production of fear.

Appropriate fear reduction strategies need not be the same in all places but should rather be responsive to the particular set of circumstances operating in each locality. Strategies to reduce the number of abandoned buildings can be administered by government agencies, while the street behavior of adolescents probably cannot be controlled by policing procedures.

These suggestions conflict with the general or abstract analysis of the fear problem, which tends to obscure variations in political context. Silberman's (1978) *Criminal Violence, Criminal Justice* is a case in point. Since we all share the potential for victimization we all are prone to the same psychological reaction. Fear is the same for all people. Differences in context are submerged into general psychological determinants.

> Ultimately, the whole fabric of urban life is based on trust; trust that others will act predictably, in accordance with generally accepted rules of behavior, and that they will not take advantage of that trust. [Silberman 1978:10]

Silberman argues for the primacy of victimization in undermining that order.

> Crime does more than expose the weakness in social relationships; it undermines the social order itself, by destroying the assumption on which it is based. [Silberman 1978:12]

Silberman recognizes the importance of local social control in reducing fear, but fear reduction comes as a consequence of reducing crime.

> Thus the development of more effective social controls in poor communities can provide a far larger payoff in reduced crime and improved order than can the development of more effective methods of policing, more efficient courts, or improved correctional programs. [Silberman 1978:429]

Echoing the founders of the social control perspective, Silberman goes on to call for local initiative in developing that social control.

> If a community development program is to have any chance of success, those in charge must understand that the controls that lead to reduced crime cannot be imposed from the outside; they must emerge from changes in the community itself, and in the people who compose it. Hence the emphasis must be on enabling poor people to take charge of their own lives—on helping them gain a sense of competence and worth, a sense of being somebody who matters. [Silberman 1978:430]

The equal security advocates challenge the "neutrality of context" assumptions of Silberman and others. Where he speaks of a generalized "fabric of urban life," we argue that the fabric of urban life varies considerably from community to community. That fabric is man-made, resulting from the distribution of values including security. Silberman may be correct that "people need to be able to make sense out of their environment," but that "need" is more or less easily met depending upon the political development of the community. Social control is a function of resources, and that makes the local social order of a concrete *political* reality, which shapes how much trust the individual can have.

It may be true that "our sense of self is bound up with our ability to control the personal space in which we live" (Silberman 1978:12). But that ability to control is not purely a psychological mechanism. It is a political capacity communities develop in varying degrees depending upon their resources.

These political capacities, however, also influence the shape and focus of reallocation formulas. Thus, the most fearful communities often do not have the resources to compete successfully for the policy benefits. Consequently, those who are most in need of better security are least capable of availing themselves of positive government intervention.

A fear reduction strategy that emphasizes community cohesion, local political development, and a general revitalization of the neighborhood should be wary of the excesses and mistakes of OEO. One of that program's major design errors was to treat the urban context as a neutral environment in which poverty reduction strategies are implemented.

If there is one implication that follows from our analysis, it is that there is nothing neutral about the urban context. Patterns of migration, local political development, the distribution of urban services, and the impact of victimization all effects communities differentially. An intelligent fear prevention program must be cognizant of the differential pressures of urban life on the generation of fear at the community level. This also means that there will be situations in which the community resources are minimal and the disorganization extensive. In these situations there is little community crime prevention can offer. The *appropriate technology* may be to protect citizens through traditional criminal justice agencies and introduce resources to improve the community's competitive position in the metropolis. To suggest that community crime prevention strategies can redress economic injustice and racial discrimination is to go beyond the theoretical synthesis we are proposing and doom the policies to failure. This is a disservice to both a promising strategy and desperate people.

References

Alford, R. 1975. *Health Care Politics*. Chicago: University of Chicago Press.

Alinsky, Saul. 1969. *Reveille for Radicals*. New York: Vintage.

Balkin, Steven. 1979. "Victimization Rates, Safety and Fear of Crime." *Social Problems* 26: 343-58.

Baumer, Terry. 1977. "The Dimensions of Fear: A Preliminary Investigation." Draft of a paper presented to Center for Urban Affairs, Reactions to Crime Project. Northwestern University, Evanston, Illinois.

Becker, Howard S. 1963. *Outsiders*. Glencoe, Ill.: Free Press. 1973 "Consciousness, Power, and Drug Effects." *Society* 10 (May):26-31.

Bell, Daniel, and Held, Virginia. 1978. "The Community Revolution." *Public Interest* 3 (Summer):142-77.

Biderman, Albert D. et al. 1967. *Report on a Pilot Study in the District of Columbia on Victimization and Attitudes Toward Law Enforcement*. Washington, D.C.: U.S. Government Printing Office.

Blake, Judith, and Davis, Kingsley. 1964. "Norms, Values, and Sanctions." *Handbook of Modern Sociology*. Edited by E. L. Farris. Chicago: Rand McNally & Co.

Boggs, Sarah L. 1971. "Formal and Informal Crime Control: An Exploratory Study of Urban, Suburban and Rural Orientations." *Sociological Quarterly* 12 (Summer):319-27.

Burgess, Ernest W.; Lohman, Joseph; and Shaw, Clifford. 1937. "The Chicago Area Project." *Coping with Crime*. New York: Yearbook of the National Probation Association.

Carey, James T. 1975. *Sociology and Public Affairs: The Chicago School*. London: Sage Publications.

Cloward, R., and Ohlin, L. 1960. *Delinquency and Opportunity: A Theory of Delinquent Gangs*. Glencoe, Ill.: Free Press.

Conklin, John E. 1971. "Dimensions of Community Response to the Crime Problem." *Social Problems* 18 (Winter): 373-84.

———. 1975. *The Impact of Crime*. New York: Macmillan Co.

Cook, F. L., and Cook, Thomas. 1975. "Evaluating the Rhetoric of Crisis: A Case Study of Criminal Victimization of the Elderly." Paper presented to School of Social Work. Loyola University, Chicago, Illinois.

Dahrendorf, Rolf. 1968. *Essays in the Theory of Society*. Stanford: Stanford University Press.

Durkheim, Emile. 1953. *The Division of Labor in Society*. New York: Free Press.

Ellis, Desmond P. 1971. "The Hobbesian Problem of Order: A Critical Appraisal of the Normative Solution." *American Sociological Review* 36:692-703.

Ennis, Philip H. 1967. *Criminal Victimization in the United States: A Report of a National Survey*. Washington, D.C.: U.S. Government Printing Office.

Feyerhern, W.H., and Hindelang, M.J. 1974. "On the Victimization of Juveniles: Some Preliminary Results." *Journal of Research in Crime and Delinquency* 11 (January):40-50.

Finestone, Harold. 1976. *Victims of Change—Juvenile Delinquents in American Society*. Westport, Conn.: Greenwood Press.

Fowler, Floyd J., and Mangione, Thomas W. 1974. "The Nature of Fear." Paper presented to Survey Research Program, September 1974, at University of Massachusetts and the Joint Center for Urban Studies of MIT and Harvard University.

Fowler, Floyd J.; McCalla, Mary Ellen; and Mangione, Thomas. 1979. *Reducing Residential Crime and Fear: The Hartford Neighborhood Crime Prevention Program*. Washington, D.C.: U.S. Department of Justice.

Furstenberg, Frank F., Jr. 1971. "Public Reaction to Crime in the Streets." *The American Scholar,* pp. 601-610.

Gans, Herbert. 1962. *Urban Villagers: Group and Class in the Life of Italian-Americans*. New York: Free Press.

Garofalo, James. 1977. "Victimization and the Fear of Crime in Major American Cities." Paper presented at the annual conference of the American Association of Public Opinion Research, May 1977, at Buck Hill Falls, Pennsylvania.

Garofalo, James, and Laub, John. 1979. "The Fear of Crime: Broadening our Perspectives." *Victimology* 3: 242-53.

Gordon, Margaret T. *et. al.* 1979. *Crime in the Newspapers and Fear in the Neighborhoods: Some Unintended Consequences*. Reactions to Crime Papers, vol. V. Evanston, Ill.: Center for Urban Affairs, Northwestern University.

Granovetter, Mark S. 1973. "The Strength of Weak Ties." *American Journal of Sociology* 78:1360-80.

Greenstone, J. David, and Peterson, Paul E. 1973. *Race and Authority in Urban Politics*. New York: Russell Sage Foundation.

Gusfield, Joseph. 1975. "Categories of Ownership and Responsibility in Social Issues: Alcohol Abuse and Automobile Use." *Journal of Drug Addiction* 5 (Fall):285-303.

Hindelang, Michael J. 1974. "Public Opinion Regarding Crime, Criminal Justice, and Related Topics." *Journal of Research in Crime and Delinquency* (July), pp. 101-16.

Hindelang, Michael J.; Gottfredson, Michael R.; and Giarofalo, James. 1978. *Victims of Personal Crime: An Empirical Foundation for a Theory of Personal Victimization*. Cambridge, Mass.: Ballinger Publishing Co.

Hunter, Albert. 1974. *Symbolic Communities: The Persistence and Change of Chicago's Local Communities*. Chicago: University of Chicago Press.

————. 1978. "Symbols of Incivility: Social Disorder and Fear of Crime in Urban Neighborhoods." Paper presented at the Annual Meeting of the American Society of Criminology, 8-12 November 1978, at Dallas, Texas.

Janowitz, Morris, and Street, David. 1952. "Changing Social Order of the Metropolitan Area." *Handbook of Contemporary Urban Life: An Examination of Urbanization, Social Organization, and Metropolitan Politics*. San Francisco: Jossey-Bass, Inc., pp. 90-128.

Keller, Suzanne. 1968. *The Urban Neighborhood: A Sociological Perspective.* New York: Random House.

Kidder, Louise; Cohn, Ellen; and Harvey, Joan. 1978. "Crime Prevention vs. Victimization: The Psychology of Two Different Reactions." *Victimology* 3:285-96.

Kleinman, Paula, and David, Deborah. 1973. "Victimization and Perception of Crime in a Ghetto Community." *Criminology* 11 (November):307-43.

Landesco, John. 1929. *Organized Crime in Chicago.* Chicago: University of Chicago Press.

Lavrakas, P.J.; Baumer, T.; and Skogan, W. 1978. "Measuring Citizens' Concern for Crime." *The Bellringer: Review of Criminal Justice Evaluation* 8:8-9.

Levi, M., and Lipsky, M. 1972. "Community Organization as a Political Resource," *People and Politics in Urban Society.* Edited by H. Hahn. Beverly Hills, Calif.: Sage Publications.

Lineberry, Robert L. 1977. *Equality and Urban Policy: The Distribution of Municipal Public Services.* Beverly Hills, Calif.: Sage Publications.

Marris, Peter, and Rein, Martin. 1967. *Dilemmas of Social Reform.* Chicago: Aldine Publishing.

McIntyre, Jennie. 1967. "Public Attitudes Toward Crime and Law Enforcement." *The Annals of the American Academy of Political Science* 374 (November):34-36.

Merton, Robert K. 1938. "Social Structure and Anomie." *American Sociological Review* 3 (October):672-82.

Miller, Walter B. 1973. "Ideology and Criminal Justice Policy: Some Current Issues." *Journal of Criminal Law and Criminology* 64:141-62.

Mills, C. Wright. 1943. "The Professional Ideology of Social Pathologists." *American Journal of Sociology* 49:165-80.

Molotch, Harvey. 1979. "Capital and Neighborhood in the USA." *Urban Affairs Quarterly* 14:289-312.

Park, Robert E.; Burgess, Ernest W.; and McKenzie, Roderick D. 1925. *The City.* Chicago: University of Chicago Press.

Piven, Frances Fox. 1981. "Deviant Behavior and the Remaking of the World." *Social Problems* 28 (June):489-508.

Podolefsky, Aaron, and Fredric DuBow. 1980. *Strategies for Community Crime Prevention: Collective Responses to Crime in Urban America.* Springfield, Ill. Charles C. Thomas.

Reiss, Albert J., Jr. 1967. *Studies in Crime and Law Enforcement in Major Metropolitan Areas.* Field Survey III, vol. 1 of the Presidential Commission on Law Enforcement. The Administration of Justice, Washington, D.C.: U.S. Government Printing Office.

Riger, Stephanie, and Lavrakas, P.J. 1981. "Community Ties: Patterns of Attachment and Social Interaction in Urban Neighborhoods." *American Journal of Community Psychology* 9:55-66.

Schneider, Anne L., and Schneider, Peter R. 1977. Private and Public-Minded Citizen Responses to a Neighborhood-Based Crime Prevention Strategy. Eugene, Ore.: Institute of Policy Analysis.

Shaw, Clifford R. 1930. *The Jackroller: A Delinquent Boy's Own Story.* Chicago: University of Chicago Press.

Shaw, Clifford R., and McKay, Henry D. 1942. *Juvenile Delinquency and Urban Areas.* Chicago: University of Chicago Press.

Shaw, Clifford R.; Zorbaugh, Frederick; McKay, Henry D.; and Cottrell, Leonard S. 1929. *Delinquency Areas.* Chicago: University of Chicago Press.

Silberman, Charles. 1978. *Criminal Violence, Criminal Justice.* New York: Random House.

Skogan, Wesley G. 1977. "Dimensions of the Dark Figure of Unreported Crime." *Crime and Delinquency* 23 (January):41-50.

———. 1980. *Issues in the Measurement of Crime.* Washington, D.C.: U.S. Government Printing Office.

———. 1977. "Public Policy and the Fear of Crime in Large American Cities." *Public Law and Public Policy.* Edited by John A. Gardiner. New York: Praeger Publishers.

———. 1976. "Victimization Surveys and Criminal Justice Planning." *University of Cincinnati Law Review* 45:167-206.

Skogan, Wesley G., and Maxfield, Michael G. 1981. *Coping with Crime: Victimization, Fear and Reactions to Crime.* Beverly Hills, Calif. Sage Publications.

Smith, Michael P. 1979. *The City and Social Theory.* New York: St. Martin's Press.

Snodgrass, Jim. 1976. "Clifford R. Shaw and Henry D. McKay: Chicago Criminologists." *British Journal of Criminology* 16:1-19.

Spector, Malcolm and Kitsuse, John I. 1977. *Constructing Social Problems.* Menlo Park, Calif.: Benjamin/Cummings Publishing Co.

Stinchcombe, Arthur L. 1978. *Theoretical Methods in Social History.* New York: Academic Press.

Sutherland, Edwin H. 1939. *Principles of Criminology.* Chicago: J.B. Lippincott Co.

Suttles, Gerald D. 1968. *The Social Order of the Slum: Ethnicity and Territory in the Inner City.* Chicago: University of Chicago Press.

Thomas, W.I., and Znaniecki, F. 1939. *The Polish Peasant in Europe and America.* New York: Social Science Research Council.

Toennies, Ferdinand. 1957. *Community and Society.* Translated by Charles P. Loomis. East Lansing, Mich. Michigan State University Press.

U.S. Department of Justice. 1977. *Community Anti-Crime Program.* Law Enforcement Assistance Administration. Washington, D.C.: U.S. Government Printing Office.

Verba, S.; Nie, N.H.; and Kim, J. 1974. "Political Participation and Life Cycle." *Comparative Politics* 6:319.

Washnis, George. 1976. *Citizen Involvement in Crime Prevention.* Lexington: Lexington Books.

Wellman, B. 1977. "The Community Question." *American Journal of Sociology* 84:1201-31.

Whyte, William Foote. 1943. *Street Corner Society.* Chicago: University of Chicago Press.

———. 1943. "Social Organization in the Slums." *American Sociological Review* 8:34-39.

Wilson, James Q. 1975. *Thinking About Crime.* New York: Basic Books.

Wilson, James Q., and Kelling, G.L. 1982. "Broken Windows." *Atlantic Monthly* (March), pp. 29-38.

Wirth, Louis. 1933. "The Scope and Problems of the Community." *On Cities and Social Life*. Edited by Albert J. Reiss. Chicago: University of Chicago Press.

———. 1938. "Urbanism as a Way of Life." *American Journal of Sociology*, 44:1-4.

———. 1940. "Ideological Aspects of Social Disorganization." *American Sociological Review* 5:472-82.

Wrong, Dennis H. 1961. "The Oversocialized Conception of Man in Modern Sociology." *American Sociological Review* 26 (April):183-93.

Zweibach, Burton. 1975. *Civility and Disobedience*. London: Cambridge University Press.

Index